Finding Refuge

Finding Refuge

a memoir

Diana Kuper

Printed in the United States of America
Cover image: Daniel Beltrán
Book & Cover Design by Mary Meade.
Edited by Judyth Hill

Finding Refuge—1st ed.
ISBN 978-1-957468-03-7

In memory of my beloved parents

Fira Birman Kuper

Mietek (Kupferminc) Kuper

"Let everything happen to you: beauty and terror. Just keep going. No feeling is final."

—RAINER MARIA RILKE

"All shall be well, and all shall be well, and all manner of thing shall be well."

—JULIAN OF NORWICH

Contents

Finding Refuge

Last Days

*Before I became a bad person trying to be good,
I wore a blue velvet beret.*

OCTOBER 31, 1959

MY MOTHER AND I SAT side by side at the Bar Mitzvah service of one of our "American cousins." Morning sun slanted down through the stained-glass windows of Adat Shalom synagogue in Detroit, the colors gracing our skin and clothes. The velvet dress I wore, a rich royal blue, featured a line of delicate white trim across my small pre-pubescent chest. Angled just so in the French style, my blue velvet beret, a darker shade of blue, rested on my long, wavy auburn hair. Eleven years old, I felt I was a young lady who already had a style of my own. The dress and the beret were a perfect expression of me.

My mother was wearing a well-made green wool dress, a cut befitting a slender woman whose high cheekbones, small nose, and dark eyes lent a Tatar cast to her face. She was one of the beautiful "Russian girls" of our Holocaust survivor community; new immigrants, "greeners," as we were called.

"Greeners" may have been a slightly pejorative term but it was also a positive identification, a term of belonging that we, the second generation, all in our sixties and seventies now, still use to mark our feelings of kinship with one another and affection for who and what our parents were and the life they built here in America. My mother's and my attire signified that we, who had only been living in the U.S. for eight years, had "made it." We wore clothes purchased on Livernois, known then as the "Avenue of Fashion," and we had recently moved out of Detroit to one of the up-and-coming suburbs newly built in the north of the city.

Sitting beside my mother, I sensed she held me in some awe— her American daughter, secure in the bland safety of mid-western, post-war America. Yet I was not "empty-headed" like the American girls but rather the progeny of European parents; a girl who knew of Tolstoy's *Anna Karenina* and was also familiar with Tatiana, the beloved in Pushkin's *Eugene Onegin*.

As a girl, back in the U.S.S.R., my mother lay on the couch which served as her bed, in the room she shared with her parents and brother. She was hungry—because Stalin had slaughtered the Kulaks who had provided wheat for the nation and now there was no bread to be found. She lay in dread of the banging at the door, the secret police, the NKVD, come to take someone away—her father, or mother, a neighbor or a visiting uncle sleeping on the floor.

My mother, well into her sixties and seventies, having lived in the U.S. for thirty years or more, quaked in fear if stopped by a traffic officer. When crossing the Detroit River for an evening out in

Windsor, Canada, she would answer tremulously when asked by the border guard, "Country of citizenship, ma'am?"

As a girl, at night on her couch, she fantasized dancing at the ball like Kitty in *Anna Karenina* or Natasha in *War and Peace*. Responding once to my query, "Mom, do you believe in reincarnation?" she replied she did not but is certain she was once a member of the French-speaking Russian aristocracy.

Her fantasies, lavish, beautiful, and comforting as they were, could never have included the more far-fetched one of herself living in America and having a daughter who sleeps in her own bed in her own bedroom. In this bedroom there are matching green patterned bedspread and curtains, wall-to-wall plush green carpeting, and a large closet with thick wooden sliding doors behind which hang different outfits for every day of the week.

This daughter, me, lies on her bed listening to a staticky Montreal radio station, painstakingly tuned to on her clock radio. She fancies herself part of the European sensibility which Montreal would have to stand in for: the cultured and romantic world of her mother's stories.

What complicated feelings of pride and envy my mother had towards me. This day I sensed pride dominated, as we sat so companionably side by side in the synagogue pew.

The older generation of our American cousins, second cousins to my maternal grandfather, were four brothers and one sister who had come to Detroit from Russia before the Revolution. During the ensuing years, through long hours of hard work, their little grocery stores had turned into supermarkets. In Europe, meanwhile, the ranks of my parents' families were depleted either by Hitler's edicts sending them to the gas chambers of Treblinka or on the battlefields of Leningrad and Stalingrad, while the family in America grew and prospered.

After the war, my parents, the remnant survivors of large extended families, and I had the legal status of "stateless persons." We needed affidavits for immigration to the U.S., which our American family kindly provided. We arrived in Detroit in June of 1951 and were swept up into their rounds of Friday night dinners and Sunday picnics at Palmer Park.

Throughout her life, my mother was engaged in a struggle with feelings of inferiority while clinging to a belief in her own superiority. The theme (her torment) was that although she was superior, circumstances, especially "the War," or perceived inadequacies of my father, brother, or myself led her to appear inferior. Although my mother may have felt gratitude and affection toward her American cousins, I never saw or heard mention of such from her. No, instead it rankled her greatly that they might consider themselves superior to her because of her newcomer, "greener" status. It was she, her thinking went, who had arrived in the U.S. with a wardrobe of European fashion they would not see for another year or two. And although she spoke English with an accent, she also spoke Russian, Polish, and German, while they, like most "provincial" Americans only knew one language. And she had a college degree while these American-born, second-generation women did not, and if not for "The War"—she would be a professional woman.

As a well-dressed guest at the Bar Mitzvah service and in the company of her American daughter, my mother was showing them "I'm just as good as you are—even better." On that day, I was able to carry the weight of this representation my mother had assigned me quite lightly, for I felt comfortable in my own skin, confident, and excited about being me.

The coming evening, I would be Cleopatra at my classmate's Halloween party. My mother and I had contrived a costume, one quite risqué for an eleven-year-old girl—a green dress made of faux silk fabric, off one shoulder and with an accompanying scepter made of cardboard and aluminum foil.

After school, that winter of my sixth-grade year, I made my way to the outdoor community skating rink. Wearing my white figure skates, short red felt skating skirt, white tights, and the white cable turtleneck sweater I wore over layers to keep warm, I imagined I was one of the beautiful blond-haired girls with their strong shapely legs skating on the frozen pond in the Bing Crosby, Fred Astaire film "Holiday Inn," the film about the farm in Vermont converted into an inn, open for business only on holidays.

My mother marveled at my identity as an American girl. In truth, it was an identity I aspired to rather than inhabited—an American girl: carefree, secure, sunny, assuming an easy belonging. Gliding across the ice in my skating outfit, I could pretend I was one, even feel that I was. American girl was appealing, but so was European bohemian girl, daring and duskily romantic. Or perhaps I was like Mary, from *The Secret Garden*, blooming, transformed, and healed by the moors and the garden and by Dickon, the boy mystic. My clothes and costumes, while social necessities and fun, were also serious attempts to express these different, dreamy moods of a possible me.

Bearing down on the serrated edge of my right skate, gaining momentum, I lost my identity-seeking self-consciousness, and gave over to the joy of dancing to the music piped in from the loudspeakers above. Round and round the rink I skated, digging in, then gliding, now backwards then forwards, twirling. Faster and faster I flew, dazzled by the music, the lights, the cold air in my face, and snowflakes like glittering diamonds floating down from the night sky.

Those were the last days of my wellbeing.

For beginning in the early spring of my sixth-grade year, four successive traumas slammed into me with force. The first two hit in rapid succession, leaving me reeling and faltering but still standing. Two more body blows delivered in my thirteenth year knocked me down and out. When I came to, I was an altered girl. A broken girl.

These days, soaring on my bike through the exalted light of spring, the wind sends the fragrance of flowering trees. I inhale deeply, a powerful life force moving through me, pouring forth in waves of joy and elation as every cell of my body sings praises of Hallelujah. My eleven-year-old skater, ice flyer self, lives in me now, this same joy and elation coursing through her. It is as though I caught up with her, my sturdy little eleven-year-old, as though I reached in and pulled the thread of her, my disrupted self, and wove it back through and up in the effort to make the tapestry of my life's fabric whole.

PART ONE

The Four Traumas

CHAPTER 1

Father

MUNICH, 1976

STANDING IN LINE AT THE reception desk, I wait my turn. The clerk, efficiently fulfilling the requests of the hotel patrons, looks puzzled, though she does not alter the polite expression on her face, when I ask for directions to the old Jewish cemetery. On a pad of paper she draws a headstone with a cross on it. I shake my head "no." Taking the pad from her, I draw a headstone with a Star of David on it.

"Oh," she says.

"The Jewish cemetery," I say.

In 1976, thirty-one years after the end of WWII, I still feel awkward and intimidated acknowledging my Jewishness to a German.

The young blond hotel clerk removes a city map from the desk drawer and marks my route on it. "Take bus #36," she says, as she puts an X on the location of the cemetery. Walking from the hotel towards the bus stop, I feel relieved. Directions to the cemetery in hand, my anxious concerns of the night before about finding the cemetery are not borne out. The pilgrimage to his grave will soon be accomplished.

This is my second visit to Munich, the city of my birth, the city where my first father died two weeks before my first birthday. Again, as during my previous visit, I feel the duty, the desire, and the compulsion to visit his grave.

I ride the bus thinking of Uri and myself. Lying in bed this morning watching as he dressed for a business meeting, I said, "I'm going to the cemetery today."

His hand rested briefly on my head, "Here's some money, you might want to get lunch as well."

Uri, our lovemaking has fallen from the heights of ecstasy. For three years I have been your adored lover. Since you divorced your wife, I am now a less desired object. I believed myself special, immune, but these days I get on your nerves like everyone else; everything I say is an irritant, everything I do grates.

The bus driver motions to let me know I have reached my destination.

"Walk two blocks to the right and you are there."

Following his directions, I find myself in front of a statue of the Virgin Mary at an old Christian cemetery. Looking at its worn stone wall, neat paths, grave plots, and monuments, and at the old gardener tending the flower beds, I want to retreat to the safety of my hotel room.

Had the hotel clerk misunderstood? Was she being malicious? World War II is omnipresent for me here in Germany. Everyone I encounter is "a German." An impulse arises, to rip off their masks, to shout, *"Why are we all pretending that nothing happened? I dare you to drop your polite veneer. I know who and what you really are."*

I also know who I am beneath my liberal, fair-minded stance. I am outraged, I am filled to bursting with rage, with horror, and with terror. The clerk's motive does not bear thinking of, I must move on and find the cemetery, and not give in to the fatigue and despair that are already creeping up within me.

An irrational thought—perhaps he will help me. I cannot leave Munich without visiting his grave.

I approach the gardener and in my hesitant German ask for directions.

"Turn to the left, walk along the river Isar, then ask again."

"Is it within walking distance?"

"It is a nice day for walking."

Did he notice that I was speaking the German of a four-year-old mixed with a sprinkling of Yiddish in what I hoped was a German accent?

My surroundings are unfamiliar. The cemetery was not near a river, I think, searching my memory from six years earlier. Walking in and out of an appliance store filled with customers, I cannot bring myself to ask directions to the Jewish cemetery in the crowded store.

Finally, I see a nun walking ahead of me. I want to stop and pour my heart out to her, tell her all that is roiling within it; make my confession, ask for her blessing. After all, some of the nuns risked their lives and hid Jewish children. I seek solace, comfort, consolation, someone to whom I can unburden myself; aren't nuns supposed to offer that? I catch up with her and ask for the Jewish cemetery. She suggests I take a taxi.

Cars in the road are speeding in both directions at a dizzying pace. I run across tram tracks to a taxi stand on the other side. Two drivers consult. "The old cemetery," I reiterate.

"Yes," says the second driver, gruffly, "the old one. Do you doubt me? I was born in Munich, have lived here all my life."

I was born here too, I think, remaining silent, for I am at the mercy of their good will. The first driver agrees to take me.

As we drive along the river through the streets of Munich, the sun comes out from behind the clouds; an ordinary summer day. We converse, I in my halting German, words emerging from a forgotten place.

"I'm glad you could help me. I feared I wouldn't find the way, and now I'm almost there." It is Uri's money and I want to be careful with it, yet I am grateful to the taxi driver and give him a generous tip.

Standing in front of the cemetery, I convince myself that it looks familiar. The gate is locked, and I ring the bell. A dog barks and I ring again. A young woman with an open, untroubled face appears at the gate, a large dog at her side, and asks,

"Do you have someone here?"

"Yes, my father."

I feel like a traitor saying those words. My father is in the United States with my mother and brother. What am I searching for here? For a father I barely knew, planter of a seed, a flimsy connection. The fact of his existence has been a burden to me; my connection to him a haunting source of the unsavory and the unwholesome. I am bad like he was.

She opens the gate. "You mean your grandfather."

"No, my father."

"This is an old cemetery. No one has been buried here since before the war."

"I'm sure it's the old cemetery, but he died in 1949."

"I think you are in the wrong place. You should be at the new cemetery, but I'll look in the book just in case."

There is no "Mendel Weisman" listed in the thick black book with its yellowing, wrinkled pages, and its black, ink-faded names.

Running across the road, I catch the bus as it is about to depart. I find my seat, consult my map, and look out the window. The gray vista the clouds left behind mirrors the pall descending upon me. I am surrounded by ghosts; the ghost of my first father, the ghost of the passionate love that Uri and I shared, the ghost of my parents' courtship on these Munich streets, and the ghost of myself, a little girl strolling between them, a hand in each of their hands. Adrift among the Germans, searching for the elusive grave, the dance with Uri ending as the music stops, I cling to the ghosts for comfort.

Uri has no patience for my moods. I should go back to the hotel and lie down, collect myself, renew my strength before he returns from his business meetings. Nothing is wrong, really. I am vacationing with Uri in Europe, as he mixes business with pleasure. From here I will fly to the U.S. to see my family. Afterwards, I will return to my apartment and job in Tel Aviv. Today I am making a courtesy visit to my first father's grave. That's all. There is nothing to be upset about, nothing. I often feel undone of late, on the verge of falling apart. The tranquilizers do not help anymore. Symptoms are taking over. It has become increasingly difficult to pretend.

A well-groomed elderly woman sits in the bus in the seat next to me. "Fraulein," she says, "You are heading in the opposite direction. You must get off this bus and go down to the train." She pats my hand with her own white-gloved one and says in parting; "Everything will be all right."

The underground platform in the modern, immaculate subway station is full of rowdy teenagers wearing the blue shirts of their school uniforms, pushing and crowding their way into the train. I find an empty seat in the corner, away from their carefree presence which rankles as my guts wind tighter.

The train car is almost empty when I reach the station at the outskirts of Munich. Following a woman who disembarked with me, I ask for directions.

"Straight ahead under the trees," she points. "I'll walk you part way." Walking side by side in silence for a pace, she then points straight ahead and turns off the street.

I pass a flower shop but decide not to make a purchase. A pleasant road, trees on each side; the cemetery is just up ahead. Coming upon it I remember entering the house inside the cemetery grounds six years earlier, in a different life. My then-husband and I, newly graduated from the University of Michigan, were backpacking through Europe. We traveled from Amsterdam to Germany by train.

A woman comes out of the living quarters and into the office. "Mendel Weisman, buried in 1949," I say. Looking through the book dated 1949, there is no "Mendel Weisman." Breaking into a sweat, perspiring and queasy, I turn the book towards me, "I'm sure his name is here, he must be here. Let me look."

I search through all the "W's" and find "Mendel Wajsman, July 1949."

The caretaker will escort me to the grave. Walking beside me, she says, "I remember you. You were here six years ago when I first came to live here. Yes, I remember you."

My then-husband and I were brought here by friends of my parents. This same woman had accompanied us to the grave site when I walked ahead of her and the others. I found my way without error then—walking along the paths straight to the grave, where I lay down on the slab sobbing, as though someone had taken over my body, someone who knew things I could not have known, someone who felt what I could not have felt. The cemetery caretaker, my husband, and my parents' friends stood back as though held by a force field, afraid to come near.

Now, hurrying to keep up, fearing to lose sight of her in this maze of graves, trees, and paths, she points to a grave overgrown with vines, the stone dirty and cracking.

"Here it is. I'll be back at the house if you need me. Now I'll leave you by yourself."

Sitting on the ground next to the grave, I sense that something is wrong. There is no crackling of connection, no recognition—a void. I move the vines away from the stone and find that it is the wrong grave, no Mendel Weisman here. Rising to my feet, I stumble among the graves in this field of graves, searching.

Throughout this day I have been in the ring boxing with demons. Are they just toying with me or are they evil intentioned? Surrounding me or within me? I do not know. If I give in to them, if I leave without finding his grave, I lose a greater battle than this cemetery visit. Surrender would take me one step closer to the collapse of my spirit, to giving in, to giving up. I will not leave until I find him.

At last. "Mendel Weisman, *geboren* 1918 Radom, Poland, *Tot* 1949," carved in German. Underneath the name and dates, words carved in Hebrew now the language of my daily life, reveal their meaning to me. "Mendel Weisman, untimely death, returned to the dust." Not "beloved husband" nor "beloved father;" only "returned to the dust."

An old Jewish custom upon visiting a grave, leave a stone atop the gravestone to mark your visit. Two stones rest on his. Did his German girlfriend leave them? Does she visit once a year on the anniversary of his death? Let it be her. Let someone come to this forlorn, desolate spot, this lonely grave.

No one comes, I know. There is no one. Only me, the daughter who wears his face, but disowns him. *You gave me life, should I thank you for that? I feel as lonely as you are. I call it loneliness, this hollow, imploded place inside me where a self should be. Though I have disavowed you, perhaps you will take pity and watch over me. At this moment the thought of you, of you being 'somewhere,' comforts me.*

I abide with him for a while.

Walking slowly, making my way back towards the entrance to the cemetery, passing gravestones, I read "Rosa Cohen, died in Treblinka," "Moshe Weiss, 30 years old, died in Bergen Belsen," "Schwartz family, died in Dachau." These are empty graves, no bodies buried underneath. Who could separate these few from the piles of corpses mounted in the camps waiting to be incinerated? Who in the outside world even knew or cared?

The caretaker stands in front of her house. "Do you want to buy flowers?"

I choose a bright pink flower planted in a brown pot. Walking back slowly past the graves of Rosa and Moshe and family Schwartz, I come to Mendel Weisman. Feeling lighter and quieter now, I place the bright flower next to him. Looking back over my shoulder, I walk away.

CHAPTER 2

Daddy

$\mathcal{M}$Y DADDY MEANT EVERYTHING IN the world to me.

That is what I was told for as long as I can remember, but it is also what I felt. He was the one who supported my head when I threw up, held me in the hospital when twenty-seven stitches were sewn into my leg, taught me how to ride a bike, called me "*mamele*" and "*cockerel.*" He was the one whose pajamas I cradled in my arms when he left for his long day at work.

I held his hand or sat on his lap at every opportunity and was known among friends of the family as "crazy about her Daddy."

"You love Daddy more than me." This was her mantra and Mom said it over and over.

"No, I don't, I love you both the same," my voice trembling, trying not to cry. If I cry she'll think it's true, that I love him more and I don't, at least I don't think I do.

"But," she added, "I don't mind."

I wasn't sure about this. Was it true that she did not mind? Was she telling me a fact, that I loved my Daddy more or was she telling me that I am supposed to love him more? Was it safe for me to pre-fer him? Could I still have her love if I did?

One February, when I was seven years old, Daddy and Mom agreed not to exchange gifts on their birthdays, which were one day apart. Daddy bought her perfume anyways, but she had nothing for him. With an aching heart, I ran to my room. In tears, I returned with my one dollar and handed it to him. Not wanting to take the money, his face registered surprise, even amusement. I raised my eyes and when he looked into them his own welled up and he took the dollar from my hand.

Daddy and I went to Montreal to visit his cousin from "home," a connection lost since before the war. Mom, pregnant, stayed be-hind. Shortly after our return, I looked up at her as she stood in front of the bathroom mirror, combing her hair. Tugging on her skirt, I begged for attention, but she continued to ignore me as she had been for what seemed like hours. Somewhere inside, I sensed this was a game we had to play, my punishment for having Daddy to myself for the week in Montreal. But how far would she carry this game if it was one? Staying behind may have felt to her like being left behind; pregnant, stewing, and resentful,

Little *Dinale*, cherished girl, lucky girl; pampered and indulged by them both. The one bedroom in our first apartment on Gladstone Street was mine. My parents slept on a fold-out couch in the living room. The little wooden table and two matching chairs just the right height for me, the shelves filled with dolls wearing pastel-colored dresses, white socks and shoes, with eyes that opened and closed, ("Daddy can't pass by a doll without buying it for you.") the collec-tion of books. We had been in America for such a short time, yet I had everything a little girl could dream of or want.

While Daddy spent long hours working, riding three buses to and from, Mom and I were companions to one another. She took me to the playground, or the park, and she read books to me over and over until I knew them all by heart. Then we had a tea party, like Mrs. Hen and Mrs. Goose, who were dressed up for the occasion in their best bonnets. And we waited for the evenings and Sundays when Daddy would be home.

Mommy, Daddy, and me; all we had was each other.

MARCH 1960

Whatever possessed me that day? Why did I go looking for the photograph of the "spitting girl;" the photo of her parents, my parents, she and I, standing in a park in New York City just days after we landed in America? The fates must have been grabbing at straws, any one would do, to push me in the direction of my parents' bedroom.

High up in their closet, propped on a shelf, was a briefcase in which I thought I had last seen the photo; black leather, nubby, with a fold-over triangular flap that buckled shut with a click. Riffling through its contents, I could not find the photo. I found old papers instead; legal documents written in German, some in Gothic script, some with English translations, printed in duplicate and triplicate on flaking paper, shades of saffron.

"Birth certificate: Diana Wajsman, born 8. August.1948."

"Certificate of Death: Mendel Wajsman, religion Israel, residing at Krailling, district Starnberg, Hans-Sachs Str. 14, died on the 25th of July 1949 at 15.45 in Munich."

"Agreement Concerning Adoption of Child: The agreement on the adoption of the minor Diana Wajsman, born in Munich on August 8th, 1948, daughter of Mendel Wajsman, who died in Munich on 25.7.1949 and of Ester (Fira) Kuperminc, widowed Wajsman, agreement on adoption of Diana Wajsman.

Mr. Mieczyslav Kupferminc adopts herewith Diana Wajsman with all the consequences established by the law. By virtue of this adoption the child benefits of all the legal rights belonging to a legitimate common child of the couple Kupferminc, married on August 18, 1950. By virtue of this adoption the adopted child receives the family name of the adoptive father and will hereafter bear the name: Diana Kupferminc, without addition of her former family name. This adoption is registered on October 3rd,1950 by attorney Dr. H. Thallmair in Starnberg and approved by the Guardianship Court."

"Birth certificate dated 16 Oktober 1950, Diana Kupferminc, born 8. August.1948"

In the early autumn of 1950, shortly after marrying my mother, my father instituted an impeccably crafted, air-tight paper trail. I imagine him carrying his briefcase, traveling by train from Krailling to Munich to Starnberg and Feldafing. He met with the attorney, the judge, and various minor bureaucrats. Every document was properly executed, notarized, and stamped with an official seal. I contemplate with a full heart the care with which my father ensured that everything would be in perfect order when we left Germany and arrived in America.

The following June of 1951, he was forty-nine years old, newly married to a woman eighteen years younger than himself, and the father of a three-year-old child. Daddy set out—the sole provider of this little family—to start a new life in a new country, foreign to him in every way, whose language he did not speak. This is when one must feel gratitude for the wisdom of how life unfolds: we move blindly into the future, one day at a time, hopeful yet ignorant of what awaits us, of what we will endure.

"Dis life is not easy to go tru, *Mamele*," he told me countless times with a deep sigh. Nonetheless, through it all he kept his promises.

Of course, seeing those yellowing pages for the first time in March 1960, I had a very different reaction. Shock was uppermost, then guilt for having searched through the briefcase, and fear that my parents would be very angry with me for what I had found. I ran down the street and told a friend the news only to return to her house again the next day to say it wasn't true. I told myself that what I uncovered did not matter, did not change anything and to just forget it.

I do not remember the rest of that evening. I assume I ate dinner and went to bed as usual. I wanted to pretend that nothing had happened, to stuff what I had learned back into the briefcase, prop it back up on the shelf in the bedroom closet and never think about it again. That was my intent.

Waking up the next morning, I was about to jump out of bed when Daddy came into my room and asked if anything was wrong.

"No, nothing is wrong."

"I think something is," he said. "you were screaming in your sleep last night."

"Nothing is wrong," starting to give way, "I want to get ready for school now."

"It would be better if you stay home today. You can tell me what is bothering you."

Bursting out in a wail and a cry, "I found out that you are not my real Daddy."

He nodded as if he had already surmised this. Still, he blanched, his face falling into a stricken collapse. Mommy and he and I would talk about it after Sammy, my little brother, went to school.

Daddy will know what to do, he already has a plan: the hope of a child for whom things were dangerously unravelling.

We three sat in the living room, Mom still wearing her nightgown and robe. I on one upholstered chair, Mom on the other, a table with a lamp on it between us and Daddy across from us on the couch. Franechka, Daddy's beloved sister, memorialized in bright colors, looked down upon us from the wall behind him.

Daddy's demeanor was serious, while Mom's caused unease. Wearing a lopsided half-grin barely suppressed; a wicked, naughty child looked out at me from her dangerously gleaming eyes. Her nose and cheekbones strained upwards with tension, revealing the conflict within—the injunction to hold back impulses and her desire to give in to them. Sensing which side would win, sensing she would leak hurtful and discomfiting words, I lowered a hazy veil. I already knew how to look without looking or rather, see without seeing.

It was difficult to meet my parents' eyes, although once I felt assured they were not angry with me, I did look to them for direction for how to feel about the shocking revelation lying there between us. I did not have to peer anxiously for cues, not at all. My parents were most unsubtle, leading me by the nose as the narrative unfolded.

I said the three of us sat down but another presence had entered the room, a man, insinuating himself into the picture.

"He was killed on his motorcycle. A three-wheel mail truck hit him. The wheel crushed the back of his skull, and he was killed instantly, although lying in his coffin he looked as though he did not have a scratch on him. Mr. Studenberg, riding as a passenger on the back of the bike, was hospitalized for weeks. He told us he ran into Mundek in Munich and Mundek asked him to come home with him on his motorcycle and see his beautiful baby daughter. They were on their way home when the accident occurred," said my mother.

The narrative continued. Mundek and Mom had a bad marriage. She left him once and went to stay with her parents in Feldafing, the displaced persons camp where my grandparents lived. She planned to divorce. Arriving at the camp on his motorcycle, Mundek talked her into going back home with him. Soon after she was pregnant with me. She was unhappy—but decided to live for her child: her child would make up for what was missing in her life.

It was all meant to be. Daddy was meant to be my father; this was the point of the story. Just as Mom's due date approached, Mundek took off on his motorcycle for a tryst with his German girlfriend. While he was gone, Mom went into labor, and I was born. Daddy was the one to notify Mom's parents that their daughter had given birth. He was acting in his capacity as the leader of the Jewish community, but this act was a harbinger of things to come.

"Mundek wasn't even there when you were born. Daddy was the one who told Grandma and Grandpa. Mundek came back when you were already three days old. And there had been an incident some months before he died. We were all out in the garden. Daddy was there too, he was holding you and when he tried to give you back to Mundek, you began to cry. Daddy teased him about it. You preferred Daddy. So Daddy was meant to be your father."

"After Mundek died, Daddy brought us food and my widow's pension. You became very attached to him and cried when he left our house. Daddy was crazy about you. I was dating several men, handsome and younger than Daddy. But I chose Daddy, even though he was much older, because I thought he would be a wonderful father for you. And he has been. So don't feel bad about Mundek."

"I don't."

I do feel bad about Daddy though. I cringe when she says it, the part about the other men being "much younger and handsome." I mean, you don't say things like that, right? It's embarrassing. It might hurt Daddy's feelings. But she is my Mom and she said it, so is it ok then?

I once asked why they told me all the sordid details that first day, when I was only a child. "We were afraid you would feel bad that he died, that you would miss him. We were afraid that you would feel differently about Daddy, not love him so much."

From that time forward it began. A malevolent genie, held tightly in a bottle for years, uncorked with much force. It seemed as though Mom forgot I was a child. She began telling and could not stop. Unleashing her tragedies upon me, I became the repository for them. Her tales were compelling, rich in every particular; love stories, war stories, even prurient details. Sitting at the kitchen table next to her, pinned to my chair—needing to use the bathroom, armpits soggy with wanting to listen and wanting to run. I stayed put even as I felt I was losing myself, even as I knew that some of her telling was wildly inappropriate for a daughter, especially a young one, to hear. "Enough, stand up, move," I said to myself, but I could not.

It was as though I was in a boat further and further adrift from the shore, unable to go back to dry land, to the self. The rope that tied my boat to hers was my lifeline; being moored to her became my survival. Drifting together in her sea of tragedy or severing the rope that bound us; there were no good choices, no real choices, only anxiety-provoking states. I no longer had my life; I had hers and mine, her sorrows and mine. First her stories became mine, then mine became hers, until there was no "me" left.

Threads of shame were woven into the fabric of my being, and they grew thicker with each sitting; shame for who my first father was, shame for the incestuous talking and listening in which my mother and I engaged, shame for the feelings evoked in me. If Mom had been a writer, things might have turned out differently. But since she didn't write, she talked.

Though I was mostly a sympathetic listener, moments would arise when my ire would be provoked, and I would try to stand up for my first father. I would look for some way to redeem him, to prove that he was not as bad as she said he was. But of course, even as I looked for an angle in which to place him in a better light, she had the goods on him while I had only conjecture. I was fighting for my life, but she did not see this nor did she understand that her words about him reflected on me.

"There, right there, when you turn your head that way and lift your finger for emphasis; it is like he is in the room," she said.

Or, in moments of anger, "You are just like him."

Tragedy was her calling card, and it became mine too.

When I was in my twenties, my therapist pointed out that I often speak of my mother's difficult and tragic life, when in reality she lives in a nice home, on a nice street, in a leafy, safe suburb, cared for by a devoted husband, and is the mother of two fine children. I was stunned. It was such a topsy turvy view of her.

It is a relief for me to know that I do not have to tell her stories here. I thought I did and I grew weary just thinking about going back to the U.S.S.R., the Stalin reign of terror, escaping from the Nazis to Uzbekistan in Central Asia, the death of her fiancé, the death of her nineteen year old brother, meeting my first father at a dance, the death of her first baby, a boy, who died in the hospital in mysterious circumstances before he was thirty days old, and the escape from behind the Iron Curtain, which was just then descending.

There are her stories, there are my stories and there is the stillness beyond stories. That is where I am heading.

But as Daddy used to say: "*Die trachts und Gott lachs.*" "You make your plans and God laughs." I could not have imagined how personal the political would become and how the events of history would thrust me back into a deeper understanding and visceral encounter with the past.

The new family

CHAPTER 3

Bullying

MAY 1960

Out past the schoolyard with its swings, slides, and monkey bars, the students of our sixth-grade class were spread out on the baseball field. We had spring fever that day in May and our teacher must have as well since it was he who suggested we go outside to play a game of baseball. Excited and relieved at this unanticipated freedom, we filed out of the classroom, talking, always talking, and laughing; toting our balls, bats, and catcher's mitts, the boys jostling one another.

Eleven years old, almost twelve now, I piled out with the others, self-consciously witnessing my happiness and joy, knowing I was well-liked and belonged. A faint shadow of the revelations of two months before hovered, but here I was, tumbling out of the classroom with the others, with what I hoped was as light a heart as I imagined they had.

Confidently taking my turn up to bat, I knew I was good for at least a few bases and probably a home run. The thick part of my bat met the ball and sent it flying far into the outfield. A fast enough runner, I was not fleet-footed like my best friend, Eva. Still, I was often the first girl picked by one of the team captains, always a boy.

I could let her have it over me, Eva, that she was the faster runner and also that her house was closer to school than mine. Her mom made mouthwatering sour pickles and baked rugelach, a delicious and delicate pastry. These counted for something in the river of rivalry, the flowing undercurrent in our friendship.

Ravenous after school, we ran to Eva's house, broke in through the milk chute when her mom was not home, and devoured half the pickle jar. Eva's mom spent her days tooling around in her little car, hitting the stores, picking up bargains. On Eva's bed lie packages of new clothes; once, an apple red sweater with a hood I especially coveted. My mom did not know how to drive a car though she kept our home clean and orderly, every room well-appointed, even the basement. Eva had a smart older brother, while mine was six years younger. Her brother and his friends definitely added to her cachet, racking up a few more points for her on the running scorecard we kept in our heads. It had to be more or less even to be friends, though one always had more than the other.

Eva said the words of our competition out loud; she always did, from the beginning. Both of us ceaselessly comparing, she gave voice to the thoughts, "you are this, I am that, my brother… your father…" whatever came to mind, telling me how I was to think of things. Still today she does it. Right from the start, I countered with a stance of refinement. I did not speak of these matters. Pretending to her and to myself that I was above such petty score keeping—who was I kidding? Not her, I'm sure, and deep down, not myself either. Still, my "refinement" gave me points, at least in my own mind.

I was the more studious of the two, a voracious reader, although our teacher told my mother during parent/teacher conferences that both Eva and I were "boy crazy." Pretty girls, evenly matched in the looks department, we wore ponytails urged into corkscrew curls.

A particular sore spot for Eva in our hapless competition was my daddy, who was openly adoring and nice to me. Hers, who worked long hours, came home late every evening carrying large packages of meat wrapped in white butcher paper, blood seeping through. The abundance of delicious meat: lamb chops, steaks, and roasts—Eva's listing of them was meant to offset the absence of fatherly affection.

She and her brother ate their dinner hours earlier and now Mr. Feldman sat at the kitchen table alone, still wearing his bloodied undershirt from work. Mrs. Feldman had cleared a space at the table for him, while she fried a large, fresh steak and pulled salad and the jar of sour pickles from the fridge. Asking about his wife's day and about the kids, he wanted to be informed, asking being a substitute for time spent together. He fulfilled his fatherly duty by working hard so that they could have everything.

The earthy odor in the kitchen, mingling smells of blood, frying meat, and sweat needed to be overcome as a slight wave of nausea rose in me. I counted points even here, though abashedly, at the same time respecting Mr. Feldman's hard work and his kind interest in me and regards for my parents. All this as I wanted nothing more than to make my way to Eva's bedroom and our young girls' concerns.

We were both children of Holocaust survivors, powerful glue for our best friends' bond. Who but each other understood how the past encroached on the present in our parents' lives, how they yearned for "home" and for their murdered families, the before and after of their lives so wrenching and utterly final. We had an unspoken protectiveness towards them and perhaps sometimes, embarrassment for their heavy accents. Stripped of everything, starting over from nothing, our parents and the survivor community had that much more to prove. They did it through us, their offspring, through our attributes and accomplishments, thus intensifying and raising the stakes of my and Eva's competitive tensions.

She befriended me on the first day of fifth grade, my first day at this elementary school. That year we were on par, but in sixth grade I edged ahead, becoming the popular girl in the class. I tried to wear it well; I know I did. Feeling proud and happy on the inside, I acted the same as before on the outside, careful not to evoke jealousy, as if I could stem the rising tide.

Two of the popular boys in the class liked me: Jeffrey and Stephen. I liked them as well but could not choose between them. I thought I would just enjoy being liked, even enjoy their rivalry and the attention they paid me.

Everything changed on a dime. It was my team's turn in the field, and I was standing near third base. Jeffrey called out to me, shouted something. Looking up with anticipation, it took a moment for me to register his scowling expression, his angry and mean words. Then Stephen followed suit. I wasn't sure what was happening and turned to Eva seeking safety in our connection. But she had already caught the drift, the shift in the wind, and turned her back on me. They said I was the "cootie" now and no one was allowed to be near me or talk to me because they could "catch the cooties." Coming out to the field, laughing together, I was the popular girl in my class. Walking back in after the game, my place in the hierarchy was dramatically altered.

It befell me, just like that.

They didn't have a name for it back then when it happened to me. The pundits weren't talking about it, you couldn't read about it in the library or online. Educators weren't having conferences on "bullying," and no one used the word on television. Of course, there had always been the classmate who was shunned, one of the "losers," in the cruel parlance of the schoolroom. I never picked on the shunned one, though I was complicit in feeling lucky that it was not me, in keeping my distance. But I had never seen this happen to one of the cool kids, the popular ones.

Hyperventilating as I walked home from school alone that day, there were black spots buzzing before my eyes like frantic bees. Panicked thoughts—*What happened? How did it happen? Don't think about it, don't think about it. But why are they being mean to me? What did I do wrong? Why don't they like me? I'm so scared.* I tried to reassure myself this would all pass the next day, but the churning, squeezing in my middle signaled to me that things were very very bad.

There were six weeks left in the school term before summer recess and I had to go. Each day, in the newly treacherous territory of the school playground—where I had once played dodgeball with the boys and sashayed around with the girls—I now swept the scene with my eyes, looking for enemy outposts, reconnoitering the positions of snipers. There were few hiding places, and I was often caught in their crosshairs.

One day, sitting by myself on a swing, a group of girls circled around me. Eva led the assault, shouting out embarrassing particulars about me and my family gleaned during her frequent dinners and sleepovers at my house. They took turns mocking me. Their desire to inflict pain and humiliation and the pleasure they took from it, a palpable presence. Instinct told me not to answer back, not to engage, to keep my gaze on the dirt under my feet, where countless children's shoes sliding back and forth had formed a groove. To wait it out until the cluster of what were, after all, just little girls, their pleasure in taunting me temporarily sated, walked away. I bore their cruelty, then faced the onslaught of my own thoughts and feelings. The mortification of being excluded, the cloak of burning shame covering me from head to foot advertising that I was *the cootie*, the girl no one wanted to play with. The sun shining down upon me felt like a searchlight, a spotlight magnifying my disgrace for everyone to see. Enduring, surviving; these were the new skills I was learning, skills I never thought I would need.

Mom met with my teacher. They arranged I would be out of school one morning and he would have a talk with the class. I had little hope of rescue. Now my life, like my parents, had a *before* and an *after*. My *before*: eagerly taking pleasure in my schoolwork, my reading, my biking, my skating, throwing the ball and my body around with abandon during dodgeball games with the boys. My *after* meant my self eclipsed: the dimmer switch dialed to "low."

My seat was moved to the other table, away from Jeffrey, Stephen, and Eva. When the teacher was in the room, the kids ignored me or inflicted vicious little maneuvers that would escape his notice, but when he had to leave the room, even for a moment, they landed on me like vultures. One day when this happened I cried. Now they had a new name for me, "Niagara Falls." I looked to one of the gentler boys, David, for sympathy but he looked away. Was he silent then or did he say a quick "Niagara Falls" under his breath just to stay in the good graces of my tormenters? He may have been silent, but I cannot say for sure.

Finally, my mother decided to phone Eva. Fearful that Eva would convince my mother I deserved all that was occurring and turn even my mom against me, I sat in the kitchen listening to Mom's end of the conversation.

Mom is my hero in this story, she stood by me and went to bat for me. She never alluded to or hinted at what I must have done wrong to have caused this. Instead, she became my champion.

"You and Diana were best friends. You slept at our house so many times. How can you do this to Diana?" I could hear Eva's flat voice, lacking in nuance, could hear her brazen reply, not the exact words but the tone.

Remembering my mother's face as she held the receiver to her ear, anger rises within me. I wonder how anger can crop up so intensely and unexpectedly after a half century. I am astonished as it ignites in my belly and rises to my chest. It might have served me well then, the anger, helped to push the cruelty out rather than turning it on myself. But I was too stricken with panic and fear to mobilize any positive aggression then.

This night, her kitchen table is littered with remnants of our dinner as we sit and talk, Eva and me. She is very thin and worn, bowed by the cancer invading her family, the demands of her role as a caregiver, and her stressful work schedule of fifty hours a week, work she will not reduce or relinquish. As it did for her father, work serves as an antidote to painful involvement. As she speaks and I listen, my heart goes out to her, she feels my love and turns towards me.

Until we begin speaking of the events told here and she says she does not remember anything except:

"They called you "Niagara Falls" because you cried all the time."

I am eleven years old again, on the verge of tears, outraged but impotent—

"I did not cry all the time, I only cried once, one day when everyone was being mean to me, calling me the 'cootie.'"

"I don't remember." she says.

I hate her imperturbability in this moment, hate that she does not care, that she dares to wound where she has already so deeply wounded, that she got away with it and does not say she's sorry.

What I want, all I want, all I have ever wanted from anyone who has hurt me is a simple acknowledgment, an empathic moment of meeting. It astounds me how rare a thing it is to receive this and yet how easily the pain and the hard place resulting from a particular incident melt into nothingness when I do.

I was not invited to the final party of my sixth-grade year, the one celebrating the end of our elementary school days and the beginning of summer recess. Sitting on my front porch alone that evening while the others were gathered a few blocks away, I listed all the parties I had been to in sixth grade. *"It's ok, there was only one I was not invited to, only this one at the end of the year. I only missed one. That's not so terrible."* Going over it all in my mind, I counted the parties one by one; thinking and counting to reassure myself, to soothe, to console.

Writing this—it hits me: *you've been doing that all along.*

Counting. Counting my people, counting my way to safety, reassuring myself with numbers. How large is the phalanx that supports me? How full is my dance card? Am I safe yet? Counting on my fingers—my friends, my family members—as if they were a cloak I could wrap around myself to keep warm. Measuring myself always by this yardstick; "they love me, they love me not."

The bullying was an act of senseless emotional violence. That is what I understand now. But my experience of it then; Jeffrey's bullying, Eva's betrayal, proved I was flawed, bad and wrong.

The bullying continued in junior high school, seventh, and eighth grade. I did not tell anyone, did not acknowledge even to myself, how shamed I felt, how the sick center of myself grew more tightly clenched and dread filled. I would see Jeffrey coming towards me from way down the school corridor and my heart would begin to pound as my armpits leaked fear. Shrinking against the lockers on the wall, I knew what was coming and braced myself for it. Or I just kept walking, pretending I was not afraid when he came upon me and shouted out "Niagara Falls" as he walked past.

SUMMER 2016

Pulling into the driveway of the country club hosting our 50th high school reunion I decide that if I see Jeffrey right now I will confront him. And there he is standing next to an available parking space.

"I want to talk to you," I say, looking up to his height but not quite meeting his eyes.

He does not know my name, nor does he remember me, but says he is of course willing to hear what I have to say.

He has no recall of the events I recount to him.

"I am sorry. I was always a bully," he says. "I did not want to come to the reunion because of it, but Eva, on behalf of the Reunion Committee, phoned me and talked me into it."

A study published in the journal of the American Medical Association in 2013 looked at the long-term psychological effects of bullying. Those who have been victims of bullying are at greater risk for depression and anxiety disorders. "We were surprised at how profoundly bullying affects a person's long-term functioning," said lead author William E. Copeland, PhD, a professor in the Department of Psychiatry and Behavioral Sciences at Duke University. "The psychological damage doesn't go away because a person grew up and is no longer bullied. This is something that stays with them."

CHAPTER 4

When Sandy
Broke His Arm

AUGUST 8, 1961

THIS IS MY CHANCE—TO RIDE the wind like the girl, the heroine in the book I read, who lives on a ranch out west. An adventurous girl who rides her horse in the wide-open spaces, galloping faster and faster. Like the girls who live in coastal towns, who ride their bikes on Main Street, fill their bike baskets with fresh bread from the bakery, who wave hello to their neighbors as they ride past—accompanied by the screeches of the seagulls swooping and careening. Whereas I, unable to fulfill the nameless yearnings within me, live in characterless suburbia, house after house after house, trees newly planted. No forest, no mystery, no nature. But I have my imagination, and I like to pretend.

I want to ride the wind, and this is my chance.

Today is my 13th birthday, and horseback riding is my birthday gift.

Sandy and I ride next to one another.

Before mounting our horses, we voiced our concerns about Bimbo, the horse Sandy was given to ride.

"He's a good horse," the two young stable hands riding along with us say, "he's fine." I'm not sure about this. Bimbo seems unruly and skittish. But what do I know? These two guys are around horses all day—I might have ridden once before in my life.

I was the one who browbeat Sandy into riding, yet I am impatient with his predicament and his fear. I need to ride faster. I signal my horse, Bucky, to pull ahead into a trot. Behind me and to my left, Bimbo reacts to Bucky's increased speed by balking and shifting sideways.

And then—Bimbo rises up off his front legs like Silver in the "The Lone Ranger," throwing Sandy off his back. Sandy goes flying, lands on the ground, his arm outstretched grotesquely in front of him.

"We'll take him to the hospital. Run, little girl, and tell his parents to meet us there," the young men say.

Stumbling across stubbly fields, unsure of the location of our cabin, my breath is ragged, and again, like the last time when the bullying began, black dots are buzzing in front of my eyes.

We are in Wisconsin on vacation with the Levinson family. Mom ordered a birthday cake for me, and after dinner, our family—Mom, Daddy, Sammy, and Grandma—along with the Levinson family, will sing "Happy Birthday" to me.

That morning, Daddy said I could have anything I want for my birthday day, and I chose horseback riding. My brother Sammy and Sandy with his two brothers joined us for the ride.

Daddy sits comfortably on his horse; I am proud of his easy manner and confidence and awed, because I have never seen this side of him. At "home," he owned and rode horses as a matter of course, although as far as I know, he has not ridden since 1939, since before the war.

We have only been riding for a half hour when the lunch gong rings.

"But you paid for an hour, Daddy. I want to keep riding."

"We'll come back for the second half hour after lunch," he says, "let's go and meet Mommy now and eat."

After lunch, everyone lounged lazily on chairs around the swimming pool.

"Daddy, you promised. You said we would go back after lunch."

"I'm tired. A half hour is enough. Stay here by the pool."

"I want to go riding. You said after lunch we will ride for another half hour."

"I said no."

As I try to persuade him to give me what is rightfully mine, a second half hour of horseback riding, my birthday gift, I am also tuning in to him as I always do; a subtext of paying attention, worrying, feeling protective, feeling sorrow for him. Is he really tired, or is it more? Is he unhappy? Is he sad? I love him with a tender, shielding love—the same love he holds for me, a mutual resonance. Although at this moment, I feel more frustrated and disappointed than tender.

It is rare, almost unheard of, for me to be at odds with Daddy. I can only remember one other time before this, last October, when I wanted to go on a hayride, an outing sponsored by the Zionist youth group, *Hashomer Hatzair*.

The summer before this one, the one after sixth grade, I went to a *Hashomer Hatzair* camp for a month with a friend, the daughter of a family we knew from the survivor community.

Camp was located in the north of the lower peninsula on the shore of Lake Michigan at Wilderness State Park. Daily life was modeled after kibbutz life in Israel. During our morning community flag ceremony, announcements were made, and work chores were assigned. We danced Israeli folk dances, sang Israeli folk songs about building the country and being built by it. We learned Hebrew words like "*chadar ochel,*" the word for "dining room." In the dark of night, we ran around the cliffs and beaches playing "Palmach and the British." Hearts pounding with excitement, we played our roles; "refugees" trying to reach shore, "Palmachniks" pulling the refugees out of the "sea" to safety, the "British" trying to capture us.

For the rest, it was a summer camp like any other; swimming, games, letters and packages from home, a talent show, campfires, friendship, and young romance. I was blessedly once again one of the gang—though not the old gang from Key School. I had a best girlfriend, and a boyfriend, and if I was not recovered from the bullying I had endured, I was at least feeling better.

One day, sitting alone high up on a bluff, legs dangling off the edge and looking down at the others playing in the lake below, I sang show tunes from "Oklahoma," "Carousel," "South Pacific," and the "The King and I." Losing all reserve I sang, louder and louder, one song after another, as if reaching for contact, calling out to the blue lake and sky. My repertoire of show tunes run through, I sat in the quiet, becoming aware of a vast, spacious stillness into which I surrendered myself.

The wildness and beauty of nature I found in Wilderness State Park filled a deep, hitherto unknown longing within me. I sought this beauty at home but could rarely find it. Ice skating under the stars was the only glimpse I had. Which was one of the reasons the hayride meant so much to me. It was an opportunity to be out in the country under the night sky, away from houses and cars and little spindly trees.

My father had agreed, despite misgivings, to send me to camp. He understood that after the bullying episode, I faced a friendless summer. When fall came, and I continued to participate in youth activities with the *Hashomer Hatzair* group, he grew uneasy. On the evening of the hayride, he drew his line in the sand and forbade me to go.

What were his objections? I did not understand. Was he concerned I would be influenced by the *Hashomer* movement and at age eighteen, announce that I wanted to leave home and join a kibbutz? It was he who hung a map of Israel above my desk and extolled the need for "our little country,"—so wasn't he grooming me for just that possibility? What then was bothering him? It seemed to have to do with the bitter struggle in Israel between the political left and the political right. Daddy had been a supporter of the *Irgun* and Menachem Begin, my mother explained; the *Hashomer* movement was way over on the other side.

Long past the starting time of the hayride, I was still begging and crying. I couldn't believe I was not going, that Daddy would hurt me, be unmoved by my tears, would put some crazy Zionist ideology above me and my happiness.

Poolside, I give up on trying to persuade Daddy and start on Sandy. Sandy does not care to go back to ride at all. He wants to swim in the pool. I badger and badger and cajole but he is holding firm to his "no" until I say, "a real man would do it."

Did I really say that? To a twelve-and-a-half-year-old boy? I thought I did. Now it occurs to me I may have confused this memory with a later one, similar words under different circumstances, said to someone else. I know that I am prone to taking on more than my fair share of blame; I may be doing that here. In any case, I prevailed upon Sandy until he acquiesced.

Our cabin is small, one room and a bath. Mom and Daddy share a bed while Sammy and I are sleeping on cots. The furniture is worn, nineteen forties rustic, the room wood-paneled, dark and gloomy. I have burst in with my news of the riding accident, and someone has gone to tell Rosa, Sandy's mom. Now the four of us are in the cabin together.

Daddy is so angry he is banging his fist on a dresser that stands in the middle of the room. He berates me for what seems like a long time and then he is yelling and crying and literally spitting out his words, "After what Hitler did to me, after what Hitler did to me, you do this to me? You didn't listen. I listened to my mother. I loved my mother. And you, I told you not to go, and you didn't listen."

He didn't say Sandy and I couldn't go, but at this point, what does it matter? It is all my fault; I brought pain to the Levinsons who are already in so much pain. I ruined the vacation for everyone.

Laying on my cot, curled up in a fetal position, my body turned to the wall, I tell my mother that I am not hungry, don't want to get up, don't want to go to the dining room. I cannot face anyone. She towers over me, insisting I must face the music, pay the price of my misdeeds.

"I ordered the cake especially for you. You will sit there with everyone who is mad at you and blow out the candles." My mother—why do I feel she is enjoying this? Is it permissible, even legitimate now, for her to be mean to me? Is she taking advantage of this moment when I have fallen so horribly out of favor with Daddy, when there is a shift in the balance which normally holds our family dynamics in place? Or is this simply revenge for shaming her in Rosa's eyes? Perhaps it is a sadistic impulse she cannot contain.

The summer before, the two families traveled together to the Catskill Mountains in New York. We caravanned for two days, and when we reached The Roxy resort, Daddy slept for another. But then he was wonderfully revived, and our vacation in the Catskills was deemed such a great success, we planned to be together again the following summer.

Why didn't we return to New York the following year? Why Nippersink in Wisconsin? It was a big disappointment compared to The Roxy with its beautiful mountainous surroundings, its strong Jewish flavor, and its slightly faded glamour.

One had to dress for dinner at The Roxy, its nightclub a venue for New York City Borscht Belt entertainers and comedians making their summer rounds. While our younger siblings were sent to bed, Sandy and I were free to stroll the grounds after dinner and then join the adults in the nightclub. In the dark, watching the show, drinking juice cocktails and dancing ballroom dances we had learned poolside, earlier in the day, it was as if we were miniature adults or children playing at being grownups. But there did not seem to be anything wrong with this, not at all; rather, one day rolled happily into another.

Nippersink in Wisconsin, on the other hand, was an out-of-the-way place surrounded by bedraggled, flat grassland. With its run-down cabins, small swimming pool, a dining room reminiscent of a kid's summer camp, and its empty evenings, Nippersink was totally lacking New York pizazz. This vacation felt like a disappointment, right from the start, yet who could have foretold what a disaster it would become and that it was to be the last vacation the two families took together.

Up to a point, there was symmetry in our two families, which warranted our traveling with one another. Rosa and my mother were two of the three "Russian girls" in our Detroit survivor community, amid a sea of women from Poland. Rosa had her parents, and my mom had Grandma. Thus, my Grandma Liza kept company with David and Clara, Rosa's parents. My brother played with Marty and Jay, the two younger Levinsons, and I was happily paired with Sandy, the oldest Levinson son.

I attribute my father always wanting what was best for his family to his willingness and choice to vacation with the Levinsons because the symmetry broke down on his line. The Levinson's dad, Lonya, remained at home when we began our long drive to the Catskills and again this summer when we left for Wisconsin.

Seven years earlier, Lonya suffered a tragic accident. He dove headfirst into Cass Lake and broke his neck. Since then, he had been sitting in a wheelchair, paralyzed from the neck down. The Levinsons were living with pain and tragedy every day. For them, for Rosa, a fall off a horse and a severely broken arm was no small matter, not "boys will be boys" but "An Accident," broken bones signifying a barely averted tragedy. My father was beside himself that my "not listening to him" had caused more grief for the Levinsons, especially during a much needed and anticipated vacation.

When I met Lonya for the first time the previous year, I felt the urge to draw back and had to force myself to step up to his wheelchair and say hello. Lonya's face was filled with ruptured veins, especially on his nose, and some of his teeth were broken and crooked. It pained me to watch him struggle as he pressed down on the arms of his wheelchair with his elbows in an attempt to shift his weight and ease his discomfort. And it was difficult to witness how he strained his head and neck upwards as if to pull himself out of his suit jacket and disassociate himself from his broken body. When I leaned over to say hello, he would raise a claw-like hand to pull me over for a kiss. The kiss never became entirely easeful for me; on the other hand, it never detracted from the happiness I felt to see him. His voice was raspy, like a loud whisper, his words humorous and witty. Within a short time after meeting, no matter his teasing, perhaps even because of it, I took the attention he bestowed upon me as love, and I loved him dearly in return.

Lonya was deeply respected by all for the life-affirming courage with which he faced his disability. He was also highly regarded for his "good head for business" and judicious intelligence.

Rosa was energetic, opinionated, intelligent, a force of nature, and perhaps formidable. At least I found her to be so. She was definitely not soft and cuddly.

She worked long hours, running the family business with Lonya and her father. Most of the "greener" women did not drive a car or, if they did, would never dream of sitting in the driver seat when their husbands were present. Rosa was in charge of the family's station wagon and later their large van. Was she a more yielding, traditionally feminine woman before Lonya's accident? Was her toughness a response to the challenges life had brought her?

I marveled at Rosa. While it seemed my parents had just enough life force to draw from to keep daily life going, Rosa had vision and energy to spare, which she used to create and enhance life, not just live it. It was a privilege to be in her orbit and gratifying to know she was fond of me. She often said, only half in jest, that she expected me to be her daughter-in-law when Sandy and I grew up.

On summer Sundays, many of the survivors would meet at Kensington Park and spend the day picnicking, swimming, and schmoozing. Sandy and I spent hours in the water, gliding over one another's bodies like dolphins; pre-teens, a boy and a girl, not sexual but edging in that direction. Loving a boy in an easy, generous, trusting way for the first time in my life, this easy loving of boys and later men became a casualty of the events of my thirteenth birthday and of the next trauma that followed eight months later.

The two families had dinner together almost every Sunday night. Rosa's mother, Clara, would cook, or we would meet at a restaurant. Sandy and his brother Marty carried Lonya out of the car and set him into his wheelchair and then we would all troop into the restaurant, commandeering a large table. No matter what occurred during the week, good or bad, I could always look forward to the warm embrace of Sunday dinner with the Levinsons.

The morning after Sandy broke his arm, such heaviness pressed upon me I could barely stand on my feet. I could not lift one leg and then another. I shuffled beside Daddy, following him around, clutching his pant leg with my hand. I had to reestablish some sort of bond, some belonging with Daddy. Absent my bond with him, I was an envelope of skin without a skeleton inside to hold it upright. Daddy had been harsh and angry with me yesterday, but today he seemed to be in normal spirits.

Sandy had a large cast on his arm and could not go swimming or do much of anything. With every glance in his direction, the white cast loomed ever larger in my mind's eye, a glaring reminder of my wickedness. Our easy companionship was gone, and I avoided him. For the rest of the vacation I kept to myself.

The Levinsons were taking another week to travel, so we drove home on our own. Looking out the window at a gray and threatening vista, I sat huddled in the back seat of our car, a new voice in my head now making itself known. The voice, propelled by a nauseous dread in my middle, tells me I am bad and wrong. Thinking thinking thinking—that new voice in my head is relentless. One thought arising after another, each one causing my innards to squeeze tighter and tighter. Or was it the dread in my middle bringing forth the dark thoughts? I strained to hold back tears that were perpetually on the verge of spilling over.

And from that day forward, I would feel this way. I would learn its name—anxiety. And depression. An ongoing, ever free-floating river of anxiety and depression. From that day forward, every day, even on the very good days, even on the happiest days, this nauseous dread—and that voice—would accompany me. Would point out my failures, my wrongs, the ways I was less than, unworthy. I would not be able to shake it off nor pray it off. There it would be, sometimes in the forefront, sometimes in the background. And it would be many years until I would have a feeling memory in my body of a life before.

Thinking about Sandy's accident, a barely acknowledged awareness arose, which, though the decision was not entirely conscious, caused me to alter my course. My desire to ride faster, my wrongdoing, must have come from the part of me that was the daughter of my first father, I surmised. He was the athletic one, the one who flew into the wind on his motorcycle, who skied down mountains. From now on, to ensure I squelch any wrong acts and any possible resemblance to him, I must banish all physical activities from my life. No more gym or ball games or skating or biking.

Wherever my thoughts carried me, there was fear and misery. I had crossed a bridge into new psychological territory. I was not well.

Sandy's Bar Mitzvah was four months later and, fortunately, right about then, his second cast was finally removed. I felt I was an unwelcome guest at the party. Rosa did not call me her future daughter-in-law anymore. And whenever we saw the Levinsons thereafter, Sandy made a remark about his arm—a smart-aleck crack or tease or allusion to not being able to play octaves on the piano. The only Levinson who still loved me as before was Lonya. I had lost the security of the loving extended "family" I treasured, the one who made up to a degree for not having aunts and uncles and cousins of my own.

One Sunday, when I was in my early twenties, we went to the Levinson's house. The grandparents had passed on, and we were a smaller crowd—the four of us, the five of them. As the gathering ended, Sandy and Rosa walked us to the door as they always did, and Sandy made a crack about his arm as he always did. My mother, father, and brother had already crossed the threshold and walked down the driveway when I spoke up. Instead of dropping my head in shame, for the first time since the day Sandy broke his arm, I talked about what happened.

Like a newly birthed fawn, legs trembling and unsteady, I stood before Rosa, seeking to explain myself. But my words did not penetrate her certainty. In her view, after the accident, I had shown my true colors; my disloyalty, my selfishness. I was not at fault for the broken arm but for ignoring Sandy for the rest of the vacation. Since her husband's accident, she stood by him, a quadriplegic in a wheelchair. In contrast, I ignored Sandy because he had a broken arm and could no longer be a fun companion. This is the lens she was looking through, the only way she could see me.

I made it down the driveway and into our car when all I was holding erupted into heaving sobs, sobs which my mother could not, would not, countenance. Her voice rose from the front seat with its nervous, agitated pitch; "Stop it! Stop it! Nothing happened!" And my brother, sitting next to me in the back seat, laughing. "You're crazy," he said.

The strange thing is memory can be deceiving. Guilt can distort it.

Sandy, at age twelve and a half, a brilliant boy, comfortable with his intellect but not so sure with his body, not athletic, not at

ease. He was self-conscious riding Bimbo, awkward in the physical realm. When my horse Bucky trotted forward, and Bimbo nervously moved sideways, Sandy decided to get off his horse. He slid
down Bimbo's side and fell to the ground, landing on his arm.

We were sixty-three years old, having a phone conversation
about the riding accident. Bimbo did not rise onto his hind legs
and throw Sandy off his back as in the memory I carried, Sandy
told me. Listening to Sandy's words, seeing, and remembering, I
watched those few seconds play in slow motion on the screen of my
mind. Bimbo moving skittishly side to side, Sandy sliding down off
Bimbo's left flank and falling to the ground.

Years later, I envisioned the events of that day unfolding quite
differently:

Bursting into the cabin, trailing panic and fear—"Sandy fell off
his horse and broke his arm!"—I am enveloped in a comforting
parental embrace. Every step of the way, each of us had made decisions setting in motion events that led to the accident: no one person's fault. I will learn from my choices and my mistakes.

It is not a tragedy, only a broken arm. Receiving help and understanding from my parents, I, in turn, am able to shower Sandy with
love and attention. Overcoming adversity, our friendship holds
firm and is even strengthened.

That is how it should have happened—if Hitler had not murdered my father's parents and siblings and their spouses and children and the entire extended family. If Lonya, Sandy's father, after
surviving the Holocaust, had not dived headfirst into Cass Lake and
broken his neck.

If. If. If.

As it was, I was thrust into the turbulence of the two families'
tragedies and sucked down into the whirlwind of their disfigured

emotions, with no chance of emerging unscathed. Sandy's injury healed, but mine was less tangible, hidden, living inside my head and body, undermining my moments going forward.

CHAPTER 5

I Risk My Life for You

SPRING 1995

MY PSYCHOTHERAPY PRACTICE WAS LOCATED in an office on the busy corner of a small, upscale suburb of Detroit. The office was rectangular, facing a large window overlooking an apple tree, that was in full bloom. One afternoon, a bright yellow bird, the yellow slightly muted by a tinge of turmeric, landed on a branch among the tree's pink blossoms. I sat amidst cool shadows darkening the room, reflecting on how I had landed here and whether I was tentatively perched or safe.

The new year had begun with the shock of a phone call from the office manager of the previous clinic where I worked. The owner had declared bankruptcy and had padlocked the door. The money I had earned the month before, during my son's winter school recess when I'd left him with babysitters, had evaporated. A sole parent and provider, I fought to keep panic at bay as I scrambled through the snow and slush, seeking a new affiliation for my psychotherapy practice. The clinic I found offered a fifty-percent split of my earnings, down from the seventy-five percent I had risen to during eight years at the previous one. All the same, we had survived the winter, my little son and I, and landed on our feet. Still, I worried about the hidden cracks in our small boat as the two of us were pummeled along the rapids of our lives, while others seemed safely ensconced onshore.

The subtleties of class distinctions had not been uppermost in my mind when I located my practice to this new venue. I was thus caught unaware when some of my patients spoke of feeling inferior, intimidated, and even resentful; feeling as though as they walked from their cars to my office through a judgmental gauntlet of well-maintained women at lunch and businessmen exuding money and importance.

Robert, sitting in front of me, was one of the patients who expressed these sentiments. A man in his late forties, he was a teacher in a suburban high school and earned a middle-class salary. But his mindset and lifestyle reflected the poverty and deprivation of his childhood. Never married, childless, he was hopelessly in love with a vivacious woman who loved another man but came to him from time to time. He had few friends. Moving through his days with a profound lack of trust, he was loathe to eat in restaurants because "the cooks scratch their gonads and then handle the food."

His people, who had moved up to Detroit from Appalachia following WWII, lived in an impoverished area of the city. As a child, Robert had shared two small rooms with his mother, father, and sister. He slept on a cot in the hallway, exposed to his drunken, rifle-toting father's coming and goings. There was no door to close, nowhere to hide.

But what had frightened him most in his terror-filled childhood, he told me, was his walk to and from school. Each morning he crossed the bridge over the Lodge Freeway onto Selden Street, a white boy entering the territory of the Jeffries Housing Projects, inhabited primarily by African Americans. Heart racing, hyper-vigilant, he would cross to the other side of the street, seeking to avoid the store on the corner of Selden Street and Gibson. This store was a particularly noxious hangout, he said, where violent toughs congregated, waiting.

As he told his story, the office floor fell away from beneath me. I was sickeningly suspended in space. Gripping the arms of my chair, I resisted where the moment was taking me—to that store on the corner of Selden and Gibson, the one my client had taken such pains to avoid, the one where my father stood behind the counter, a lone, pale, white face. I saw him wearing a short-sleeved lightweight shirt over a sleeveless undershirt, his thinning hair combed back from his forehead, his refined, shapely hands working the cash register.

MARCH 14, 1962

I am usually asleep by now, but tonight we tarry, my mom and I. She sits on the edge of my bed as I gingerly lie back against the pillows, searching for a comfortable perch on the hair rollers encircling my scalp. I talk animatedly about the goings-on of the day in my very American junior high school, playing up the happy moments, keeping up the charade of my carefree girlhood. It is now 11:10 p.m. on a Wednesday night, and Daddy will be home from work in another 15 minutes, so I may as well wait until he arrives before I settle in for the night.

The phone rings. This is the shrill noise in the night's silence I have always dreaded—dreaded and expected. My youthful mother, whom Daddy ruefully but with affection calls the "teenagerel," jumps off my bed and runs out of the room to pick up the receiver of the beige wall phone in our kitchen. I hear a shout, and as I run down the hallway catch a glimpse of her grabbing her coat from the hall closet and bolting out the front door. The phone is still dangling from its cord in the kitchen.

"Mr. Policeman, Mr. Policeman, this is the daughter," I say, "is my daddy alright?"

A male voice answers, "Just tell your mother to hurry." But mother has gone, has run next door to ask our neighbor for a ride downtown to Receiving Hospital.

My brother Sammy, seven years old, wearing boy pajamas with a pattern of cars and trucks printed on them, comes out of his bedroom.

"What's wrong?" he asks sleepily.

"Daddy broke his arm in the store, a box fell on him, but he is alright. Go back to sleep."

I tell this lie, knowing Daddy is not alright. I want to protect Sammy, and I fear that I will be unable to take care of him if he starts to cry. Fortunately, he is reassured by my words and returns to his room and to sleep.

The impact of that night was physical for my daddy, of course, but also for me. It was an intense body blow shattering my nervous system, reconstituting it into a quivering mass of neurons poised at high alert. As I waited through that interminable night while my mother paced the floors of Receiving Hospital and my daddy fought for his life, a trembling terror coursed through me, causing me to run to the bathroom and urinate every few moments.

Which explains what happened when I talked for the first time, at length and in detail, about the night my daddy was shot. I was in the office of my Jungian analyst Devorah, a survivor of Auschwitz, a sallow-skinned woman, taut and wiry. In my mid-twenties, living in Tel Aviv, I sought Devorah's counsel as I was beset by unrelenting anxiety and depression.

A year or two into my analysis, I dove into the story of that night, seeking to garner Devorah's approval as I spoke. As if the events of that night belonged to her and not to me, and if I delivered them to her in the right packaging, she would give myself back to me, absent the fear and suffering. I wasn't quite sure what she wanted in the way of a presentation. Overly emotional would not do, I sensed, but then, an account devoid of emotion would seem pathological.

In hindsight, what I desperately needed as I sat in the leather armchair in her consulting room was warmth, comfort, and kindness, but warmth had not been forthcoming. She was a German Jew, tightly wound, formal and correct. And I, who had not received warmth or comfort from anyone during the events of that dreadful night nor its aftermath, had not known to hope for it or seek it or even understand what I needed.

The telling moment of my narration of the experience of the night of March 14th, 1962, turned out to be what happened after I left Devorah's office. As I walked back to Uri's new salmon-colored Audi, a Chanukah program had just ended. The parking lot was crowded with cars full of parents and their children. I pulled out of my parking space into a log jam of cars. Waiting for traffic to clear, I felt the building pressure of an irresistible urge—followed by an explosion—an avalanche of feces and urine pouring into my green corduroy pants, down my legs, over my green and white knee socks, and into my navy-blue lace-up shoes. I propped my arms on the steering wheel for ballast, raising my haunches above the seat in an effort to spare the new Audi's upholstery. When I arrived at Uri's apartment, he, to his everlasting credit, did not concern himself with the soiled seat of his car; instead, he helped me into the bathtub and bathed me tenderly.

My father and his business partner purchased the store at 1336 Selden Street, "Selden Patent Medicine," in the late 1950s. By the 1960s, the nearby Jeffries Projects, eight fourteen-story buildings built in 1953, had become a drug-infested haven for dealers and users, making the store part of a high-crime area in a city destined to become the murder capital of the world. While the Selden Patent Medicine store provided over-the-counter medicines, cigarettes, milk, candy, soda pop, and other sundries to the inhabitants of the Projects, for all intents and purposes, it was a liquor store.

Looking for a way to support his family, my dad walked into the Jeffries Projects and into the tragedy of race in America. He had never seen a black person before coming to the U.S. He knew nothing about Black history or about the ravages of racism. Daddy suffered the deadly antisemitism of Europe and now, in a twist of fate, he was cast as a White Man oppressor spending his days and nights as a foreign transplant on this racially combustible soil.

Days and nights—because the store was open every day of the year except Christmas. Daddy and his partner took turns working there—a 7:00 a.m. to 3:00 p.m. shift followed the next day by a 3:00 p.m. to 11:00 p.m. shift. Our family life and my parents' social life revolved around this schedule. Mom, when she received an invitation to a dance, or social gathering, would walk over to the calendar with trepidation and hope, marking off the days: morning, afternoon, morning, afternoon, was it Daddy's turn or Sigmund's to work the night of the dance? "The store" made the life we led possible, paid for everything we aspired to, and yet we held it in resentment.

On the night of March 14th, 1962, it was Daddy's turn to take the afternoon shift. The day's cash take, folded into gray cloth bags, was ready to be deposited into the safe when the gunman entered the store at 10:45 p.m. He ordered my father to hand over the bags. As Daddy bent down to turn the money over to him, the robber fired his gun, and as Daddy ran, a bullet struck him. This is the version of events my father told me—a brief, one-time allusion.

The newspaper account taken from the police report differs, describing two clerks held at gunpoint in the back of the store as the gunman called out to Daddy, who was standing by the cash register, to bring him the bags of money. Daddy ran away, and the robber fired three times, striking Daddy once, and fled without taking the cash.

"Kuper ran," it says in the newspaper, as if he were just some guy named "Kuper," not the father I held so tenderly in my heart. I was haunted by the image of him running—by the mercilessness of that moment. I felt ravaged by his aloneness and by his fear, undone by his vulnerability.

Early in the morning after the shooting, I heard the side door opening and hurried over. Mom, no longer the youthful woman of the evening before, stumbled through the door, propped up by a male relative. Without glancing in my direction, she moved past me, half-carried to her bedroom, where she remained for the rest of the morning and into the afternoon. I looked in on her several times, listened to her sighs and laments, but she did not concern herself with me. Daddy would have held and comforted me, but he was not there. He was the reason for our anguish, not its solace.

I have always held the moment when my mother walked past me against her. No words of comfort or reassurance, no hug, not even "hello." Her thirteen-year-old daughter had passed a night as nightmarish as her own. Did she think she was the only one to suffer?

This brings to mind an afternoon when my mom was in her eighties. The two of us were walking arm in arm, round and round the perimeter of her condominium complex, trying to keep one step ahead of the anxiety threatening to engulf her. She was afraid of death, and we were trying to outpace it. I listened and responded and listened some more to her dark and fearful thoughts, meeting her fear with the love of a daughter, with the skill of a psychotherapist, with the spiritual teachings in which I was immersed. Nothing I said soothed her for more than an instant. Finally, exasperated, I turned to her and said, "Mom, we are all going to die; it is a natural part of life. I am going to die too." Her head swiveled to face me, her look one of utter astonishment. We continued walking in silence. My claim to my own existence, separate from her suffering, had startled us both.

In the operating room, the doctor lay down her instruments —my father's heart had stopped beating—the doctor later told my father and mother. But he fought for his life, and would not give up, so she picked up her instruments and resumed the operation. His concern for my mother, brother, and I was the bedrock of his existence; even the surgeon acknowledged this. He had to live, for he knew we would be helpless without him. The strength of his devotion, his ability to survive (yet again) should have reassured me, instead, my sense of security was completely undermined. From then on, I knew we were vulnerable, our existence precarious.

Each day when I phoned the hospital, his condition was reported as "critical." And then, one day, they said his condition was "stable;" he would live.

A bullet fired from the gun of a drug-addled bandit.

On the surface, it seemed that everything had returned to normal. We were a family who loved one another. We continued to live in our nice house on a nice street. Mom and Dad resumed getting dressed up and going to dances. We went to restaurants and movies as before. Holiday dinners remained holiday dinners, friends around the beautifully appointed table, the food abundant and delicious. Daddy went back to work at the store, though never again at night.

I have seen how we humans hold on to the form of our lives after disaster has struck, how we foster and nurture the form and treasure it anew. The familiar brings such comfort and reassurance, and we cling to it with the hope of erasing the violence of our misfortune. As soon as possible, we are back in the old routine, the worst only a memory. Only a bad dream lurking, not damage revealing itself, cropping up in unexpected ways.

Driving along Northfield Boulevard in Daddy's car, Sammy and I were laughing at the sound of the word "Vaati," the name for "daddy" in German. "Vaati," we laughed, "Vaati." The sound of the word seemed hilarious to us, this first time with Daddy back in the driver's seat. Suddenly Daddy's face and body twisted with rage, and the car swerved up onto the boulevard. Not long afterward, at home, my brother made a silly remark. Daddy flung his teacup filled with hot tea across the room, shattering it against the wall. And sometime after that, Sammy lay on the floor, Daddy kicking him with shoeless feet until I put my body between them.

This was nothing like the father we had known before.

We did not understand what had happened to him. PTSD was a phenomenon that had not yet been identified and given a name. The awareness of it was not yet ubiquitous in our culture. For my father, it was like this: he had survived Hitler only to be shot in his store in America. It took the passage of years and the mellowing of age before he returned to his previous, gentle comportment.

When Daddy came home from the hospital, his best friend and his wife came to our house every evening to give Daddy a massage. The friend asserted, and everyone agreed, it was high time for my mother to learn how to drive. Look how helpless she had been asking for rides every day for the three weeks Daddy was hospitalized. So the best friend, "an intelligent man," my mother said proudly, began to give her driving lessons before administering Daddy's massage.

When this friend's mouth was smeared with red lipstick after one of those driving lessons, I hastened to alert my mom before they entered the room where my dad was lying in bed, and his friend's wife was sitting in a chair beside him. "Well, what is so wrong?" Mom wondered aloud to me later. He finds her attractive, they were only kissing, and after all she has been through, she deserves something nice, some interest taken in her.

"Daddy is not the same since his accident," my mother told me when I was fourteen. Her averted gaze and downcast eyes letting me know she was confiding a sexual secret: "The surgery affected something."

Mom has an admirer who invites her to dance at their survivor community parties and phones her in the afternoons when Daddy is at work. "What's wrong," she wonders aloud to me, "if we talk about running off to California together?" After all, she is much prettier and more intelligent than his wife—of course he would dream of running off with her.

"Would I come along?" she asks me.

"Absolutely not."

Mom acts blithely, oblivious of consequences. It is just a phone relationship, a comfort in her boring housewife's routine. She sits in the basement on the white metal chair in front of the iron mangle. She feeds the freshly laundered sheets into the mangle. They emerge on the other side, pressed and smooth. She is wearing her housework clothes, an old shirt, and baggy pants. But in her mind she is not in the basement at all. She is dancing, dressed in the black silk dress which clings to her body, wearing her black satin high heels and carefully chosen jewelry. He invites her to dance, many of the men do. She is desired and beautiful. Now she guides the tablecloths into the mangle. Daydreams and fantasies keep her going.

The sordidness of trysts in hotel rooms, hot suburban sex like in Updike's novels was not her way. In her day, movies ended with a kiss, the screen fading to black. Only speaking on the phone, or dancing in his arms. It was like in the movies, innocence preserved. More would be asking too much of her, would be too much like life, not dreamy at all.

It is Sunday and we are at Kensington Beach, in the area frequented by the "greeners," the Survivor community, the area furthest from the water and closest to the parking lots. I am sitting on our family blanket when Mom's admirer walks over. As he talks with my mother —was my father there as well?—he tosses grapes, one after another, down onto the blanket, aiming for the upside-down V between my crotch and my crossed legs.

Since my father was shot, I had come more heavily under my mother's influence. I had slid imperceptibly towards her, switched my allegiance from my father to her. I loved my father as fiercely and protectively as before. Yet the vulnerability I perceived in him made her seem the safer bet.

CHRISTMAS DAY, 1963

We are gathered to celebrate the arrival from Israel of Daddy's only surviving family member. Those present are those most dear. They raise their glasses for a celebratory toast. Daddy's face looks rested, his impeccable brown suit gives off golden lights. The others in the room fade into the background. Daddy is the one I see. My gaze is on him alone. I rejoice in his happiness, at the youthful glow in his eyes and face—when the trembling terror of the night he was shot creeps up my torso and hijacks my thoughts. I cannot trust the happiness of this moment. Daddy is going to die. I will lose him. Love means losing, not having but losing. Fear shadows my love, and this shadow will haunt my ability to love others in the future.

"I risk my life for you," Daddy said when he was angry with my brother and me. What was I to do? It was true. He risked his life for us.

OP Man Shot, Holdup Fails

A 60-year-old Oak Park man was critically wounded Wednesday night during an unsuccessful holdup attempt at his patent medicine-liquor store in Detroit.

Morris Kuper, 24221 Scotia, underwent surgery this morning at Receiving Hospital, Detroit, to remove a bullet from his left chest. His condition is "critical."

Detroit police said Kuper, part-owner of the Selden Patent Medicine Store, 1336 Selden, and two clerks were in the store about 10:45 p.m., when the gunman entered.

Police said the man held the two clerks at gunpoint at the rear of the store and called to Kuper —standing near a cash register at the front of the store—to bring him the money.

Kuper ran, police said, and the bandit fired three times, striking Kuper once. The gunman fled without the money, police said.

Kuper, who has two children, has lived in Oak Park for five years.

Royal Oak Tribune, March 16, 1962

PART 2

Ann Arbor and Tel Aviv

CHAPTER 6

School Days

1964

$\mathcal{S}$ITTING AT MY DESK, I resolutely turned my focus to the textbook lit by my desk lamp. I resisted the muffled hum of television seeping under the closed door, the enticing sounds of a movie my parents and brother were watching in the living room. It was frustrating to let the minutes tick by and allow the plot of the film to unfold without me, my chance to see it slipping away. But there was the declension of the French verbs I needed to memorize, and I still had to unravel the puzzle of the geometric structures in the pages of my math textbook. Also, a social studies term paper waited to take shape under my pen. Steadfastly striving, I hoped my diligence would bear fruit.

For I yearned, I absolutely needed, to secure a place for myself in the incoming freshman class in the fall of 1966 at the University of Michigan. This was my junior year of high school, and I had catching up to do if I wanted to be admitted.

Ann Arbor, my City upon a Hill, was the place where my true life would begin. There I would find others like me, those who were also "too sensitive," and read books like Koestler's *Darkness at Noon*. I would find others who "read textbooks for fun," as my brother said of me. Yes, at the University of Michigan, I was sure I would find others who thought about the things I thought about and felt what I felt.

I had visited the campus only once and recognized it immediately as the place where I belonged—or to be precise—the place to which I badly wanted to belong. Ann Arbor elicited an intense longing, as though who I was meant to be was ensconced there, just out of reach and I needed to go there and claim myself.

But first I needed to overcome the less than stellar grades of the year before, when I often did not show up at school at all.

In the early autumn of my sophomore year of high school, I fell ill with pneumonia which I contracted shortly upon the heels of a major embarrassment brought about by my father.

On Yom Kippur eve, the traditional fast having begun hours earlier, our family walked home in the solemn dark following the *Kol Nidre* service. Entering our home through the side door leading to the kitchen, we were welcomed by the warm light of memorial candles, protective sentinels glowing on the kitchen counter, candles my parents lit in memoriam to their lost families.

Perhaps to avoid hunger pangs or any temptation to eat or drink during the fast, my father went to bed early. Our house settled into a quiet hush. Suddenly the ringing of the telephone broke the stillness, and I ran to grab it. This was an answer to my prayers, a boy I had a crush on for the past year was calling to invite me to be his date for the Homecoming Dance. But my father, woken out of a deep slumber, picked up the other line and, before I could say a word, yelled at the boy in his broken English, "Who is this, who is this? Ahhh, you go to hell." Within seconds the line went dead. I was left holding the phone, mortification spreading through my body. The remorseful chagrin my father expressed the next morning only hurt my heart more as I could not bear to see him in pain. Nor could I countenance the kids at school after the boy spread the word about the phone call, making fun of my dad and his accent. And without a date, I was left behind at home the night of the dance.

Sick in bed with pneumonia for three weeks, I received a get well present from my parents, a beautiful powder blue peignoir set, an extravagance fit for a bride. A glamorous garment worn by movie stars, those goddesses of Hollywood, Marilyn Monroe, Ava Gardner, and Elizabeth Taylor, with their big breasts and curvaceous hips. I did not have the sex goddess curves to fill the negligee; my fifteen-year-old body disgraced me with its puniness compared to the ideal.

Also, I had a problematic and queasy relationship with my body due to severe dysmenorrhea. In our school bathroom, I lay down on the floor, pressing my belly against the heating duct, seeking relief from painful cramps. Each month, my body betrayed me for several days, diarrhea and nausea causing me to devolve into a smelly, groaning, crying mess trapped by my sinister womb.

The two-piece blue peignoir with its sheer nightgown and negligee—I wanted to inhabit it, to be graced by its glamour. The garment was beautiful but impractical and problematic. The blue nylon material irritated my skin while the elastic bands around the short puffy sleeves pinched my upper arms. The voluminous folds of fabric, bumpy and scratchy, made finding a comfortable lying down position impossible. Worst of all, the nightgown was completely sheer. The flowing and alluring peignoir coat gave some cover due to its abundance of fabric, but the ensemble was, for all intents and purposes, completely transparent.

Was I meant to wear this while bedridden and come to the dinner table like the Emperor in his New Clothes, rising above these bizarre circumstances? I did not sashay into the kitchen like Loretta Young—though the peignoir certainly merited sashaying. I just hoped the beautiful peignoir would stand on its own and allow me to merge into it somehow, making my body inconspicuous and my ridiculous nudity invisible to my family sitting around the dinner table.

The only way I could manage was to withdraw from myself, deep into the body. To pull my eyes inward as though not seeing could help me not to be seen and withdraw from the confused feelings the situation engendered. The mound of repressed emotion I pushed underground did not lie quietly though. Rather, it was like the dirt under a rock, dirt filled with slimy worms and insects actively moving and heaving, sending up shoots of self-loathing and revulsion.

It was not just the peignoir. It was also the sensation of being wound ever more tightly in the shroud my mother was wrapping around me. Contracting pneumonia put me in her thrall, in her purview, under her control. She was haunted by fears of my biological father's mother and brother's near-fatal bouts of tuberculosis. Now I was ill, in her mind, with a lung disease, and must totally turn myself over to her care to survive. She ministered to my needs with devotion, giving me what she had longed for: a mother who did not have to go to work and would not leave me at home, sick and alone. Didn't I understand how fortunate I was?

Returning from the Sweet Sixteen party of her friend's daughter, my mother, enlivened by her outing and smelling of fresh air, sat down on the edge of my sick bed. I hoped the pleasure of getting out of the house for the afternoon and being "between people," as she liked to say, would have satisfied her, and protected me. But after a few moments, I felt it coming: the stealthy approach of innuendo.

"Barbara looked so beautiful today." she said, "She has a beautiful figure and wore a perfect outfit for the occasion. Everyone talked about how charming she is, so cheerful, friendly, and outgoing. She is such a good daughter, so close with her mother, gives her so much *naches*."

I try to match my mother's good cheer, try to take her words at face value. Yet I feel, as I have so many times before, diminished by her words and her oblique delivery. I sense the comparison with Barbara, or any number of girls, the daughters of her friends or girls she hears about from her best friend Shirley, who knows and talks about everyone. Mom remarks on every best quality of every one of these girls, expecting me, I feel, to match and transcend them.

I imagine her sitting at the luncheon table with the other mothers at the Sweet Sixteen party, her superiority not acknowledged. And not receiving compliments about her daughter—who is sick in bed at home, not chipper and cheerful at all. And though Mom has begun to notice I am compromised in some way, and she may even have some guilt about what might have caused this, still she resents me as her image was not fed, and she suffered a narcissistic injury. Now I will have to pay. Or perhaps I am imagining all this, perhaps these are my feelings of competition and inferiority and not hers. Perhaps she is only sharing her happy afternoon, even trying to cheer me up. I am not certain of her intentions and have only the queasy feeling in my gut to go by.

When I finally returned to school, I felt buffeted and assaulted on all sides by the clanging metal of slamming lockers, the rush of students filling crowded hallways, and different classrooms, desks, and faces every fifty minutes. A gauzy veil separated me from the others—feelings of being less than, insubstantial, and the sickening dread oozing through my body.

Even though the pneumonia had passed, it felt safer and easier to stay at home, to seek comfort in novels, in eating the meals my mother prepared, and in her presence. I could not, however, relax with a big *Ahhh!* and settle into safety. Instead, I felt hounded by the schoolwork I was missing and the life of a high school student I was running away from.

For many days, sixty in all that school year, staying home was the best I could do.

After one particular nearly weeklong hiatus, I returned to school to find, unbeknownst to me, my biology and history classes were scheduled for tests that day.

Velma Potrude, my biology teacher, was not swayed by my "A" going into the test or my protestations of illness. "It is up to the student to find out what was missed." she said in her firm, neutral voice. My body flushed hot with dismay and tears as I filled in the very few answers to the questions I knew. It was not only the pain of the D I would receive on this test in a subject which had become important to me. As I sat there grieving over the entire mess I was in, I realized I had been betrayed. One of my best friends, with whom I spoke on the telephone nearly every evening, chose not to mention the tests we would be given. The difficulties I struggled with did not bring understanding or compassion from her. Rather I felt the smarting sting of her judgment, her disapproval, her unspoken "What the hell is the matter with you? Why don't you get it together?"

My history teacher, more merciful, gave me permission to take the test the following day and was kind enough to offer a ride home from school in his car. He stopped the car on a side street near my house and exacted a wet, slobbery kiss on the lips before he let me go.

Tenth grade lives in my memory as one gray, fearful day after another. I slogged through thick molasses, heavy limbed, and heavy hearted. When anxiety threatened to overcome me, I crawled into my bedroom closet and sat on the hardwood floor, my back against the wall, knees tucked up to my chest. The safety and stillness of the small, enclosed space held my suffering such that I momentarily felt able to bear it.

"I want to see a psychiatrist." I told my parents. "I don't feel well. I need help."

My mother did not need to voice her shame of me. It was enough she phoned a different cab company each time I needed a ride to my appointment. When I returned she asked if the sessions were helping and how many more I would need, as these visits were placing a financial burden on the family. Several months later, "the help" ended in betrayal when my mother, after meeting with the esteemed doctor, informed me, a triumphant look in her eyes,

"He said your problem is you are jealous of me."

Perhaps? But what about the post-traumatic fallout from the violence perpetrated on my father, what about my guilt and feelings of worthlessness following the blame heaped upon me when Sandy broke his arm or the bullying I had endured? Were my problems, in any way, related to the "sessions" my mother and I were having where she spoke of the misery of her life with my first father and the disappointments and unfairness of her life now? And could the cause of what brought me to his office simply be the hurdles of adolescence? None of these were the reason for "my problem." None of these had any merit in the eyes of a psychiatrist who was psychoanalytically trained and looked for signs of the Electra complex under every rock.

With the hope of help now gone, if I was to survive and not succumb to the suicidal thoughts which surfaced, I needed to reach deep down inside myself. It was a matter of will, of courage, of my animal nature, prompting the placement of one foot in front of another. It was imagining scenes of future fulfillment, fleeting visions of a possible life ahead.

I sought to teach myself how to live. I did not sit down and make a list of what to do or how to do it, I just carried on. I gave my best—galvanizing my inner resources, shackled to the ball and chain of my anxiety and depression that hobbled and sometimes crippled me.

Spring arrived, and I took a shaky step into a dance at school. It was there I met a tall boy who leaned down towards me, who even from that first moment gazed at me fondly. A drooping eyelid and slightly skewed lip left over from a childhood bout with polio broke up the symmetry of his face and distracted from the beauty of his blue eyes. He was the student council president, one year ahead of me in school. I was flattered by his interest, but more important, comforted and reassured by his presence. My mother liked him right away—this was the kind of boy she had dreamed about for me. I told him what my mother said about him, that he was not Andre Bolkonsky, the cad, but Pierre Bezuhov, the kind one, the one who Natasha married and with whom she found domestic bliss. I felt so fortunate to have met Ken. I was grateful for his friendship and kindness toward me. One summer evening, we drove downtown to see the film "My Fair Lady." Going on a date in his parents' car, listening to classical music on the radio—after the difficulties I had been through—these moments felt delicious to me, as though we were wrapped in a magical haze. And the way the evening ended—Ken and I standing on a pier overlooking the Detroit River in the quiet dark— I had someone I trusted, someone I could tell while we stood there that my parents' marriage was in trouble, and my father talked of chucking it all in and leaving for Israel.

So I made every effort to ignore the gnawing disappointment of not being, in the parlance of the time, "turned on" by him. Not only not turned on, but sometimes irritated or repulsed, like when he rubbed my palm with his finger as he held my hand. I could only hope attraction would spring forth as fondness and friendship deepened.

Spring turned into summer, into August, and my Sweet Sixteen party. The photos show a girl surrounded by friends, wearing a white dress with a flower at the bodice, every hair of her long, shiny mane perfectly in place. The photos do not lie. They show what is real, celebratory, even fun. It looks so good, who knows, maybe it was, maybe I was ok, maybe I was fine. Only, just perhaps, I was not.

That autumn was the beginning of my junior year of high school, Ken's senior year. The Sadie Hawkins dance was upon us. If I were fine, would I have invited his best friend instead of him to be my date? Would Ken have stood in the doorway of my French class, hurt and outrage sparking from his face? Would he have pointed a finger at me and shouted, "You are mud, absolute mud!" If I was indeed fine, would I have needed this pain and drama, this face-burning reminder of my badness, this cruel hurtfulness my crooked heart unleashed on another?

I spent my senior year determined to be normal, to be an all-American girl. The role I played was not who I was or even who I aspired to be, but it seemed to be the only game in town in my middle-class suburb of Detroit. It was a positive identity I could at least simulate: the refuge of normalcy. All A student, active in extracurricular activities at school, college bound, I had a wholesome boyfriend, a boy next door type. I attended the high school football and basketball games, danced at the school dances. Finally, all my efforts were crowned in the spring of my senior year with the glory of an acceptance letter from the University of Michigan.

CHAPTER 7

Ann Arbor

SEPTEMBER 1966

University of Michigan, Ann Arbor

A CO-ED, I WALKED ALONG THE lane behind the Diag, just past Ulrich's bookstore on my way to Denison Hall. The early fall day was overcast at the University of Michigan, one of the most beautiful university campuses in the Midwest. The promise of new beginnings filtered palpably through the air. The promise of new beginnings for all except for me, that is. Classes had begun three weeks earlier, and I was feeling dreadfully ill, separate from everyone, enclosed in a chamber of uninterrupted, constant disease and fear. Waves of anxiety surged through my body relentlessly and intolerably, poisoning all the moments of meeting my hall mates, eating in my dorm's cafeteria, walking down the hill to class, buying textbooks in the bookstore. The students walking by to the front, side, and back of me, lived, it seemed to me, in bodies aligned with their aims as they moved forward with their student lives. Not me; my body-mind system was malfunctioning.

I found a seat in the auditorium of Denison Hall. The lecture for my Introduction to Sociology class commenced, but I could not concentrate and did not have a context for what the professor was saying since I had been unable to focus on the assigned reading for this or any of my other three classes and was now hundreds of assigned reading pages behind. My anxiety rose to unendurable heights, and I stood up from my seat and left the lecture hall.

After three weeks of this, I was ready to give up what I held most dear if only I could make the pain stop. I was even willing to leave Ann Arbor and go back to bland suburbia. I was ready to return home if only I could have a moment of relief—and that is what I did. It was as though the movie of arriving at my dorm, Alice Lloyd, waving goodbye to my parents, arranging my belongings, and setting up my room, was now playing in reverse. I packed, carried my suitcases and boxes out of my dorm, placed them in my dad's car and the three of us Mom, Daddy, and I drove home.

I managed to salvage the year by reinstating my acceptance to Wayne State University in Detroit, where classes were about to begin, and I completed my freshman year course work there.

What was the cause of this collapse? The endurance system I had honed for myself as a response to the fallout of the four traumas was not enough to sustain me. It could not bear the pressure of the demands of my first year at college away from home.

I did manage to return to Ann Arbor the following autumn of my sophomore year and was able to hold on this time. Had I been shadowed by an observer, walking with me along my days, she would have reported I was living the expected life of a University of Michigan co-ed, class of 1970. But inside, I knew I was enduring, not enjoying, struggling rather than living, suffering, and slogging through the gray film that surrounded me.

Until, that is, the spring of my senior year, when I sprang to life. My bicycle had a basket in the front. I don't know why this brought a feeling of happiness, but it did. What was it about a bicycle with a basket, about jeans and a tie-dye T-shirt and long hair flying out behind me? I wanted to shout out to the heavens, voice my joy for this novel feeling of liberation—riding my bike up a long hill over a bridge, across a river, even in the rain. This was me, me, riding past houses, each one different from the other, riding through streets lined with old trees, some paved with brick, me—moving through a landscape that had undulations and a bell tower, an evocative landscape I had known before only in books. I felt so deeply stirred, so grateful, so wanting this never to end.

Twenty-one years old, a senior at the University of Michigan, I had come back to life for the first time since I was thirteen.

My life circumstances in this spring of my awakening were not perfect, simple, or even good. I married the wholesome boy next door, my boyfriend, from senior year of high school. But he was no longer the bright, cheerful, optimistic, 4.0 and pre-med student he had been. Following his mother's sudden and premature death, which occurred our freshman year of college, and his father's subsequent slide into alcoholism, my husband was unraveling. He rarely attended classes, his grade point slipped and then plummeted drastically, and he succumbed to a romance with marijuana, mescaline, and LSD. Possibly worse—although I would have to say it was the drugs—he also succumbed, a mere two months after our wedding, to a sexual relationship with a woman. And their sex took place in our bedroom, in our bed, during the afternoons when I was student teaching in a nearby town.

How to explain the good feelings those days brought me, when our relationship was damaged and one year later would end in divorce? Despite it all, I was happy to be alive.

I wore a new uniform, a hippie one (although I believed I was beyond all uniforms). A *fashionista* no longer, I owned my first pair of jeans. I was free to wash my hair and let it dry without blow dryers and endless pampering. This was not simply a matter of time saved or of being newly secure in my appearance without primping and preening, nor even about conforming to my new values of "being natural." It was about how l was closer to the earth now, closer to the river, able to feel the wind on my skin, to expand beyond my body, no longer locked away in a tight container.

Could I have this? Could I carry my belongings in my bike basket? And, arriving on campus, put my bag over my shoulder—my body for the first time feeling like it belonged to rather than represented me—and walk into Mason Hall? Was it really me who sat on the Diag with friends and received the sun? Me, who had a dog named Speedy, a little ruffian taking on the big dogs, my husband and I jokingly referred to on the Diag as "the guys who follow Speedy around." Me, who was valued in encounter groups and among my friends for being sensitive, transparent, and willing to share my emotions. Me, who was not suffering, at least not as before, who felt pleasure and who belonged to the Age of Aquarius, to something beautiful.

Our friends gathered at Jeff's house and then made our way to the Centicore Bookshop, which was open well into the evening. This was the beginning of my lifelong pleasure of spending evening hours in bookstores with friends or alone, filling myself with future reads and mind travels. Knowing that as long as there are good books, there would always be a source of happiness for me, and life would be worth living or at least bearable. We wandered out of Centicore and moved on to the ice cream store next door; mint chocolate chip was my new discovery and favorite. Across the street, on North University, was a movie theater that showed art films. "Elvira Madigan" was the movie we watched. My senses were filled with Mozart, with the slow scan of a bowl of sweet cherries in cream. I languished in the Danish countryside, the bees buzzed so close the hairs on my arms stood up and when I stepped out of the theater into my own spring night, the leaves on the trees rustled above me as my bike glided home under the stars.

This upsurge of living was over within months. The last class to complete my B.A. ended in June, friends left Ann Arbor and dispersed to the next phase of their lives, and my husband and I returned to Detroit. Soon after, I left him and moved to my own studio apartment. I found a job working at a mortgage company, becoming an assistant to one of the vice presidents, a Mr. G. I spent my days among people who had watched the sixties on television rather than lived them, who damned those hippies and college students. I was lost to myself again, my brief glimpse of living the life that was within me over for now.

Fall turned into winter, into spring, and then it was summer. My boss, Mr. G, had a florid complexion that was turning bright red; "It is an irresponsible thing to do, to leave," he said. "I am teaching you this business. You are taking on greater responsibility and will be promoted. Why run off like an irresponsible hippie?"

Why was I giving up the opportunity to learn the mortgage business? Why quit, for what? The office life, these concerns with setting up mortgages for homebuyers, had merit, I was certain. But it was as alien to me as if he was insisting I remain in the northwest, in a lumberjack camp sawing down trees—honest work, but did it suit me?

I did not know what to do. I did not know where to go, I did not know who I was.

But I definitely and thankfully knew who I was not.

The familiar "alone in an empty Universe" dread-filled anxiety followed me out of his office, a reaction to the doubts and criticism he raised, a response to his disapproval. How dare I follow a smidgen of a knowing within, telling me I had done the right thing and that somehow I would be led to the next step in my life.

Back in Ann Arbor, adrift for the summer, I had the idea that I might travel to Israel and learn Hebrew. Studying, being a student, was something I knew how to do. I seized this postponement, this temporary reprieve from adulthood—for which I felt and believed myself to be woefully unprepared.

Diana 1970

CHAPTER 8

Yonatan and Uri

1971–1978 TEL AVIV

*I*N LATER YEARS, IN MY forties, closed in by the gray skies and the little houses, row upon row of them plunked down on small lots in the working-class suburb where I lived, feeling alone and thwarted—I turned to the memory of Yonatan and me in the car, rain pounding ceaselessly, as we made our way down from Jerusalem.

I hailed from Detroit, where cars were ubiquitous and readily affordable for most, but for the past two years, I had been getting around Tel Aviv by foot and bus. I had come to share the Israeli yearning for cars which were heavily taxed, highly coveted, and a sought-after luxury. Sitting in Yonatan's car, protected from the rain and secure in his carefully adept navigation of the mountain roads, my sense of him as representing security, comfort, and belonging was enhanced.

Yonatan shifted the engine into second gear as the car wound down the twists and turns of the road from Jerusalem to Tel Aviv, making its way to the coastal plain.

"Let us marry; we will make a good life together," said Yonatan, his eyes peeled on the slick road.

"But we don't have a sexual relationship." This had been unspoken between us for many months—and finally speaking this aloud was awkward.

"My parents have what I would say is a very good marriage, although without passion," still not looking at me, was his reply.

I wanted to say, "Yes, I will marry you." I loved him without question. But I was not in love with him. I knew I could not lie next to him night after night, a looming absence filling the space in the bed between us. The days would be good, but the nights would be false, a sham, a charade, and I knew I could not do it.

The gloomy rain and my weeping were a sodden response to the hopelessness of a situation that tantalized without giving satisfaction. Sour bitterness rose from my chest to my throat, my tears an inadequate expression of the railing against fate roiling within me. Why did it have to be this way?

I longed to belong, to find a home in this land where I was a new immigrant, to find my place somewhere on this earth. Each day required the effort of learning a new language, and a new culture. Each day, I had to make my way through a physical environment nearly as foreign to me, who came from the placid U.S. Midwest, as Outer Mongolia might have been. My Hebrew had actually become quite good, constantly improving and refining, as I kept company with Israelis who were intellectuals, writers, and poets. Yet my accent was heavy and instantly marked me as a stranger; even the clerk in the grocery store spoke to me as if I were a small child with a limited vocabulary. Yonatan's proposal offered sanctuary and respite, a hearth radiating warm, gentle heat on which I could rest my weary body.

Kindness, empathy, and intelligence poured off the whole of Yonatan, as well as out of his eyes. He had a way of listening intently, turning to me with an open mind and open heart, listening and speaking with attentive sympathy. I did not know then how rare this quality was. I may have had the hubris to think what I said was exciting, fascinating, and merited such attention. Still, I did know to value and appreciate what I was receiving and to love him for it. He loved me for the right reasons, for what I valued in myself, calling me a *"tipus mitlabet,"* one who questions, a seeker. He was not threatened or suspicious as some of my other new friends in Israel were of my undefended way of sharing myself. With him, I felt safe. So, why could I not be in love with him? Why could I not say "yes"?

We met through mutual friends, a circle of extraordinary Israelis. They were the *crème de la crème* of the upcoming generation, born like me in the year of Israel's independence, 1948. For the past year, I had spent Friday evenings in their company—my head spinning, enchanted, dazzled by their beauty, their repartee, their spontaneous recitations of poetry, or acting out the dialogue of a play. Though there were also the less appealing cockfights, when the men argued politics or literature, voices raised to outshine one another with their brilliant wit. Occasionally, a woman would join the melee, hoping to be taken seriously, but was quickly shoved aside. Late into the night and early morning hours, positions became more extreme, while rounds of coffee, sweets, and nuts were brought out on trays, one round after another. I had never seen anything like it and felt so privileged just to be in the room, sitting next to Yonatan, who often sat listening quietly and sometimes offered a few sage words.

We sailed and swam, hiked and toured, and held one another, trembling in resonant emotion, when, at the cinema, "The Last Picture Show" ended. Perched on a stone wall on the heights of Belvoir Fortress, a Crusader castle in the north of Israel, Yonatan pointed out sites in the terrain below. He narrated their history as though he had been there, as in some way he had, rooted to this soil and this land as he was. I wanted to belong too, to stake my claim through him.

The quickening of all my senses up on the heights faded when we returned to the car in the car park below, and there I felt it again, a slight distaste, an inner recoil from his small hands on the steering wheel of the car, and the tic of his sniffling nose and curling upper lip, a mannerism inherited from his mother. I needed him to embody his slightly pudgy form more fully, to fill it with his manhood, with his strength, the competence and mastery he personified when steering the rudder of his small sailboat on the choppy waves of the Mediterranean Sea, a stance which drew me to him but was not sustained in the way he carried himself ashore.

He was twenty-four years old, perhaps a late bloomer. I, however, was already divorced, a bit taller than him, slim, holding a higher ranking in the hierarchy of outward appearance of our respective genders, which still mattered quite a lot, back then, when we were young. Yet this would not have been of consequence had he known how to carry himself, had he the confidence to take me into his arms, woo me, make love to me, and allow himself to be carried by his love and passion. But that was not his way, deeply feeling though he was. We were soulmates whose bodies seemed to be superfluous or did not enter into the equation. Love, yes, but without Eros.

The psychologist with whom Yonatan consulted after his unhappy experience with me reassured him that he was fine; I was the problem, not him.

Each morning, Yonatan's mother woke up vigorously attacking the day—relishing her role and tasks in the family enterprise, dressed in her no-nonsense business attire and serviceable shoes. His father, a more gentle presence, worked alongside her, and both the business and the family flourished. There were interesting dinner guests, often from abroad, gathered in the dining room of their home in a sought-after suburb of Tel Aviv. Yonatan had gone to a prestigious high school and had been a paratrooper in an elite unit in the army. He had not struggled with psychological symptoms; he was not lost and ever seeking. His parents did not sit in their nightclothes and lament their lives.

URI

The evening we met, Uri arrived at my friend's apartment and asked that we join him for dinner and dancing at a bar in a neighborhood of Tel Aviv I had not been to before. During dinner, Uri and my friend bantered and joked. Their conversation overlaid on a bed of irony; quips and witticisms seemed to serve as a mask that concealed the person underneath. What was amusing for them was alienating to me. I sought distance by vacating the surface of myself and pulling inward, away from their conversation, away from the rather unsavory atmosphere of the bar and from the unseemly notion of two young women having dinner with an older and married man. I compared Uri to Yonatan: Uri is unwholesome / Yonatan is good and pure. I sat in the dark bar, longing for the cleansing light of the Galilee from which Yonatan and I had recently returned.

Until, that is, Uri invited me to dance and took me into his arms for the first time. He surprised me with his gentle, even diffident holding of me, and with the tender kiss he planted on my forehead.

One balmy spring evening a month or so later, following dinner at a French restaurant where Uri was known and warmly greeted by the owner, he and I walked along the seashore, caressing breezes wafting over us, and then made our way to his hotel and up to his room. Early the next morning, wearing the white silk pants and halter top of the previous evening, I stood under the hotel's portico waiting for Uri to bring his car around, feeling quite sophisticated and grown up. As I stood waiting, Yonatan's father drove past on his morning commute to his office, located nearby. I tried to block out this was actually happening—as though if I were invisible to myself I would not be seen by another. But he looked hard, right at me and my shame and mortification were intense. This was the woman his son brought home for Friday night dinners, who had intellectual discussions with his other guests. It is not what it seems, I wanted to shout out to him. Uri and I are coming to know one another. Why just the evening before at dinner I spoke to him about the imperative of self-transparency in creating relationship. Oh God, how I wanted to disappear; how I wanted to have chosen the life that Yonatan represented.

Uri came to town unexpectedly, surprising me with tickets he had secured to the new film then the rage in Europe, "The Last Tango in Paris." A film filled with fleshy scenes of Marlon Brando and a voluptuous Maria Schneider, that bordered on the pornographic. Yonatan and Uri passed one another on the stairwell to my apartment, Yonatan coming down from another talk with and rejection by me, Uri coming up the stairs, tickets in hand.

I wanted to see the film. Uri wasn't corrupting me. I wanted him, wanted the sexual awakening I had been dreaming about, to wait for Uri when he arrived in Tel Aviv each week and ran up the stairs to my apartment. I wanted him to pull me into his arms, my back pushed up against the door as it shut behind us, my heart plunging to my stomach, my stomach plunging to my knees, Uri kissing me and trembling. Every nerve ending in my body was hyper-awake to this new erotic landscape. The pleasure laced with pain of his comings and goings, his marriage and the two little girls, the impossibility of it all, the skin of his face next to mine, the ecstatic moans of his husky voice arising from deep within his belly; all exquisitely heightened my pleasure. He was an experienced lover, yes, but what we had together was not mere sexual gymnastics, not raw sex. Uri's warmth, his tenderness, his unbridled loving expression of feeling affected me so deeply and bound me to him, ruining me for any other man. I loved his bones; I did. I thrilled to the bones of his wrists.

Uri returned to the city where he lived and worked, to his newly built home and successful engineering firm. A son of former kibbutzniks, who grew up in worker's housing near Haifa, he distinguished himself as a member of a new upper middle class in a country still characterized by long rows of apartment blocks populated by government clerks making middling government salaries. I returned to my routine; work, studies, grocery shopping, socializing with friends. In a lucid moment, I sat down and thought—*There is still time to get out, you know. Look at what you are doing, you are writing a check that will be cashed one day; you will have to pay for this. Are you sure you will have the emotional funds to draw from when the bill comes due?* I did not want to listen to this voice which knew I was heading for more than I could handle. Knew this was folly, too big for me, as though life was one of my beloved novels and I, the heroine in it, heedless of what might befall me as long as it was a good read.

Those first months of our love affair included a weekend at a resort in Eilat, the sand burning hot. I had not yet grasped the ferocity of the sand of the Middle East and did not bring my sandals down to the beach. Reclining on my towel reading, a shadow crossed over, and I looked up to see Uri, who had returned from the hotel room and stood above me, my sandals in hand. This gesture, his kindness, felt personal, relational. It pointed to a level of feeling and connection I had not expected. It transcended the stereotype of the younger woman engaging with an older, well-established man, each enamored by what the other represented.

Several weeks later, on our way up to Jerusalem where Uri had business, we stopped for lunch at Abu Ghosh, an Arab village. Seated on the terrace overlooking the vista below—a dreamy haze of sunlight, terraced fields, and the light green leaves of ancient olive trees—the beauty before me registered in my perception, and I wanted to give myself over to it. But I was held in the thrall of my emotions with the accompanying bodily sensations that claimed me, pulling my attention away from the landscape spread out before me, and towards my passion for Uri. Even in his presence, I missed and longed for him. All my antenna tuned his way, as if I was merely the vibration left over from the ringing of chimes, not substantial enough to be an entity in my own right.

Still, on this day at Abu Ghosh, in the beginning, when I realized I was falling in love, I found the wherewithal to say —

"You have two little daughters, and I am falling in love with you. It is best if we part."

"You would leave me all alone?" he asked.

I was resilient enough then that as the days and weeks passed, I found I was living well without him. I had returned to relishing the novelty of life in this city hugging the shore of the Mediterranean sea. The sun refracted off white buildings against blue sky, each day providing newness and discovery—when he phoned and pleaded that I meet with him. He said he was going crazy with longing—all he saw on the television screen was my face—he was lonely and bereft without me. He had left his wife, he said, and taken an apartment in Tel Aviv. It was always half-truths, I found out later. He had taken an apartment in Tel Aviv, true, but had not left his wife. And finally, when he did leave her and obtained a divorce, he never could or did marry me.

Six months after we met, the Yom Kippur war broke out. You can believe all the novels you have read, and films you have seen, about wartime, about the London Blitz during WWII, for instance, and how people clung to one another in a carnal life and death embrace. He drove up to Tel Aviv late at night from somewhere in the Negev desert where he was stationed underground in the hidden bunker of Central Command. Telling me only after the danger had passed, how he had seen on the monitors, at the beginning of the war, that the entire Sinai Peninsula was empty of Israeli forces. "The Egyptians could have marched right up the peninsula straight to Tel Aviv if they had wanted to," he said, "nobody was there to stop them."

How could I, an American girl from the suburbs, brought up on romantic stories from literature by a childlike mother lost in fantasies and dreams, resist this real-life drama of a man driving hours in the blackout, headlights turned off, to be with me for a short while in the middle of the night, wearing his wartime khakis, smelling like himself and good sweat? Driving all this way to hold me in his arms so I would not be alone in wartime, in this war that had descended on all of us.

Events during those years had an irresistible poignancy. One was not just living one's own little life but was caught up in the fight for survival, in the currents of history, the personal and the historical in fact converging, and no matter how many times he told me the story over the years about the night when he was fifteen, and his father woke him with the news that the United Nations had voted for partition, for a Jewish state; he would cry. And of course, I would cry too.

Uri was a Francophile of the first order and engaged a French tutor to help him learn the language. We listened to French songs in the car. "*J'attendrai,*"—"*J'attendrai, le jour et la nuit, j'attendrai toujours, ton retour,*" a nostalgic pulling at the heartstrings kind of WWII song and Uri, swaying the steering wheel to and fro, rocked and danced the car between the lanes, singing to the music. We flew to Paris—some business, mostly pleasure—pleasure I was able to have, hold and savor, especially the laughter.

Have I mentioned the laughter? His sense of humor, absurd, hilarious, an acute sense of the ridiculous, leaning towards the misanthropic. Walking through the *Bois de Bologne*, Uri glances over at a row of people sitting on benches leaning up against a whitewashed building, their faces turned up to catch a few rays of the winter sun just emerging from behind the clouds. A woman reaches up to touch her husband's head, straightening his sparse hairs blown by a breeze, "Look at them sitting there, just look at them grooming like monkeys."—a throwaway line, a clipped inflection, and I couldn't help laughing. I had never laughed with anyone before, this joy and fun that he brought me, the jokes with the Yiddish punchlines. I may have been a foreigner, an American, but I knew my Yiddish and could appreciate his humor. I hoped, I felt, and wanted to believe that this familiarity would endear me to him even more, creating an unbreakable bond between us, and he would always want and need me by his side.

I analyzed and dissected—could all this be the unconscious acting out of my personal history? Perhaps the two of them, Yonatan and Uri, reflected the split within my psyche, Uri representing my biological father, Yonatan, my loving and tender Daddy. Uri, the sexy adulterer, Yonatan, the steady, devoted, tender man whose love I do not deserve; such went my musings. My mother's pupil, I learned to crave drama, to run from the ordinary, to run from the possibility of being trapped like my parents in a life of necessity. I preferred to create my own troubles, so life would not hit me with the "real ones." Whether this was true love or raw passion or the acting out of unconscious psychological issues, it took over my life until I could think of nothing else. Living for the nights, the acute ecstasy and suffering of this romance, was a drug I craved and to which I was addicted.

Several years later, it is mid-morning, and I am bathed in cold sweat, paralyzed in fear on the bed. Uri and I have argued once again. He yelled and blamed and before he slammed down the phone receiver, said he is not coming to Tel Aviv today and does not know when he will be back. Abandoned, a vast desert of emptiness surrounding me, I am an outcast accused of wrongdoing and banished from the tribe, sent out to the wilderness alone, left to die of deprivation and loneliness.

Mounting panic, thoughts racing like terrified rats running wildly, boomerang against the confines of the cage of my mind. My ear is cocked to the phone in the other room, waiting for it to ring, for him to give me a reprieve, to hear words like "it is not you, not your fault, I am just tired and irritable, don't take what I say to heart." Words that would grant me amnesty, would bring me back to the land of the living. But such kindness, the possibility of such reassurance is not forthcoming, and I am damned to be cut off, with no ability to reach him, punished and afraid to move.

It started as one more argument of many since Uri, guilt-ridden and miserable, had divorced. It was not for him to be a divorced dad who takes the girls for the weekend, who needs to prepare food and entertain them in his spare apartment, which is not home to the girls or even to himself. He is exhausted, stressed, and anxiety-ridden since the Yom Kippur War. Its aftermath took its toll on the Israeli economy and diminished what had been his thriving business. He has child support and alimony to pay, is responsible for maintaining two households, and must face his heartbroken, humiliated ex-wife and the crushed little girls. And then there is me as he sees me now—immature, demanding, hysterical, unbearable.

We are meeting friends at the annual Israeli book fair at City Hall Plaza. The publishing houses and vendors with their tables full of books fill the square, which is surrounded on all sides by restaurants, cafés, and falafel stands. I feel the uneasiness of a dissatisfied Uri at my side, feel him like a physical force, a mass pushing against me as my unease rises, bracing myself for the eruption of his angry, blaming words. He is hungry, and it is my fault that we are standing out here, meeting friends. When Nili arrives, she says to him, "What is the matter with you? What do you want from her? Just go to one of those," and swings her arm in an expansive arc around the square, "go to one of those places and get yourself something to eat." I hadn't thought of this, that he could take care of his hunger on his own, that I hadn't done anything wrong, that this pressing buildup of his discomfort is not mine to fix.

On a Saturday afternoon, our group of friends gathered at Yael's house, the children running around, an abundance of food. Varda has read to us from the newly written chapter of her novel in progress. Uri arrives with his girls, the three of them clearly ill at ease, especially the younger daughter, who appears compromised in some slight way. They make their way into the gathering, and he introduces them but does not say hello to me, does not acknowledge my presence in any way. "You have someone here," Nili, again Nili, says to him remonstratively.

He feels as though one burned from head to toe in a tank during the war, he says, and every touch hurts. He screams in pain and lashes out at all my insensitive touches. Of course, it is the blame, the blame, that kills me—and I feel increasingly unwell. Struggling to keep going, to function, I am caught in a vicious circle. I believe all he says about me—I am wrong, bad, impossible, selfish, deserving of yelling and abandonment. Yet in this climate of anger and blame, I cannot mature in my loving, cannot put my own needs aside as I would like to do, cannot put his obvious pain foremost. I despise myself for not being selfless, not meeting my ideal of love, instead, scrambling to hold myself together, defending myself from his rage and the ugly mirror he holds up to me. I continue to cling and look to him for salvation, to love me as before. Which only proves he is right in all the accusations he hurls at me.

I am frozen with fear, leaning in my bed, unable to lay back on the pillow or sit up.

My friends come to my apartment and consult with one another. They decide to phone my psychoanalyst Dvora, who asks to speak to me and tells me in her matter of fact, unemotional voice that I have two choices. Either I get out of bed, or she will hospitalize me.

Hospitalization, the threat of it, makes the cold air in my room seem more ominous than before. I fear hospitalization more than the onslaught of emotions waiting for me if I move out of my frozen stance. I inch my legs over the side of the bed and allow my feet to hit the floor, then walk slowly and haltingly to the bathroom. Holding my body as if following a prolonged illness, frail and shaking, I step into the bathtub leaving the door open while I shower, requiring that a friend stand nearby. My body feels like an unknown object I am required to soap and wash and rinse, every movement of my arms and hands taking everything I have.

YONATAN AND URI

I left Israel after seven years of my sojourn there; "*Yaradetee*" as they say in Hebrew, not "left" but "went down." When Yonatan came to say goodbye, his disappointment in my leaving was palpable. I felt ashamed of how my leaving looked to him—I was abandoning the project, the Zionist dream of building the country and being built by it. I saw in his eyes, or so I projected onto him, the lowering of myself in his estimation. I felt this whenever we met in the following years—like when I stood over the crib of his firstborn daughter, I unmarried and childless, or when he asked if I was still, *still?* involved with Uri. I relished these little humiliations. My penance and punishment, my just desserts for having rejected and hurt Yonatan, for having been at fault and having made mistakes, for my unworthiness.

The missed opportunity with Yonatan became a club that I used to beat myself. Especially as he went on to marry, have children, become wealthy, and travel all over the world. He went on to live life to the fullest, a life I could have shared with him. He lived it without me.

I assumed I knew what Yonatan felt about me, what his judgements and thoughts were. But Yonatan had his own version of reality, and he shared it with me in an email following my visit to Israel in the winter of 2011:

"Your response to my question, *How would life have looked for us had we stayed together?* moved me deeply," he wrote—"your openness, your clear-sighted vision; I already know what it is that I have been missing… The question, *How would it have been for us?* does not usually occupy me as I go through my days, but when I see you I wonder, and I feel that I missed out on something essential. For me, ours was both a deeply intimate emotional relationship and also sexual attraction that wasn't actualized. Obviously, I was very disappointed that you weren't attracted to me. For sure I was too young, lacking experience and self-confidence. I don't believe that there is one of us here who is 'guilty' in the failure of the relationship. I certainly don't blame you and I also am not really guilty. It was a matter of timing. I met you before I felt secure in myself, in my desirability or my sexuality. The conditions for our relationship did not present themselves then and falling in love is a matter of chemistry, that's how it is, what can you do? I am definitely happy with my wife and children, but I never had with anyone else a soul connection and the desire to be with someone all the time, as I had with you."

I had used the ending of my relationship with Yonatan against myself. Judged myself as bad and undeserving. I tormented myself for having made a mistake when I refused him—until I changed my mind, and the story of Yonatan underwent revision. It all seems so simple now. Of course, I could not marry Yonatan. I was not attracted to him, and he was not embodied in a way that allowed him to express his physical love for me. That is all.

But is that true?

Or, Or—was my ability to love a man as damaged as my nervous system? Did I experience irrational, unexplainable aggression towards men who were kind to me, men who cared about me?

The me Yonatan appreciated and loved was not apprehended by Uri, not needed, or wanted, not relevant. It is stunning, really, how two people can look at the same thing and see something so different. Could the woman who Yonatan loved be the same woman loved by Uri?

Who was I in all this?

Diana, Wilderness of Zin, 1973

CHAPTER 9

Muktananda

When I left Ann Arbor in August of 1971 and migrated to Israel, I moved not only through space but back in time, leaving behind the dawning of the New Age in America.

I entered the zeitgeist of Israel, where, in 1971, the country was only twenty-three years old, the socialist economy was struggling, and soldiers were dying daily in the War of Attrition.

The cultural revolution of the sixties in America: pot-smoking hippies questioning authority, turning up their noses at a prosperity only dreamed of by Israeli youth, protests against the Vietnam war, Sensitivity Training groups promoting self-transparency and emotional vulnerability, Ram Dass speaking at Hill Auditorium about being here now—all this so dear and wondrous to me, appeared to Israelis as not only hopelessly naïve but even dangerous.

The Israelis who became my dear friends were secular and intellectual. They included me warmly in their families and lives and were drawn to my otherness, but my "counter-culture" sensibility, though met with a small ingredient of fascination for anything

American, was also resisted with a large dose of hard-nosed realism, skepticism, and scorn.

As the years passed, Ann Arbor—with its festival of student-hippies spread out on the Diag lawn playing music, causing my Irish creative writing professor, watching the spectacle through the windows of Mason Hall, to proclaim, "There is hope for America yet"—became a fairy tale to me, a receding dream, as I immersed myself in my compelling Israeli experience of love and war.

In the summer of 1977, six years into my life in Israel, I returned to the U.S. for a visit and traveled to the Bay Area to visit friends from my university days. They had left Ann Arbor several years after I did and had recently bought a home in Piedmont, near Oakland. Diane and David were excited to show me their newly purchased mansion which, Diane explained, had previously been Muktananda's ashram. I knew nothing of "ashrams" or "Muktananda" and found this information to be so "California," exotic and luxurious. Diane apologized; some of the rooms were not yet redone and I would be sleeping in one of them: in Muktananda's bedroom on his mattress, the room still painted the deep purple color he had left it.

During my visit with Diane and David, I relished a sustained sense of enjoyment, ease, and an unfamiliar light-heartedness, which I attributed to my friends' graciously enfolding me into their magical California lifestyle. It did seem a bit odd to me though, my hand caressing the cherry wood banister, as I floated down to breakfast each morning, to look down and notice the molecules of the wood vibrating and shimmering in the sunlight pouring through the windows.

And it did seem strange, since gardens had been a matter of indifference to me, to feel myself drawn to the vegetable garden in the landscaped yard behind the house. The garden glistened with quickened light as though tiny fairies beckoned, seeking to make themselves known to me. Dancing and laughing they ushered me into the garden, waved me forward, and urged me to pay attention, to truly look and see the red of the tomatoes growing on the vines, the knobby skins of the cucumbers, the lush green bouquets of lettuce; to become aware of the teeming life that dwelt there. The aliveness, the powerful life energy you find here, they seemed to be saying, this same energy dwells in you, in your own being.

Back in Tel Aviv, a city built on dunes hugging the sea, square cement pavers underfoot cover the sand, creating sidewalks on Yehoshua Bin Nun Street. As I walk past one plain, unadorned, white apartment building after another, I hear the sounds of radios from the open windows, the familiar *beep beep* announcing the hour and the news, the reassuring voice of the broadcaster reading the events of the day, and the musical notes of children practicing piano, violin, or clarinet—all bearing witness to the lives being lived inside the apartments on both sides of the street—a hubbub I loved and treasured.

Tel Aviv is the same since my return to Israel—but I am not. If a play of my life had been mounted on stage, before my trip to California, I would have said that an Auschwitz scene of emaciated prisoners wearing their ragged striped uniforms would be the most telling backdrop. Though I reveled in the vivacity of Tel Aviv, the ultimate influence upon my psyche was Auschwitz. But now, as I am walking along Yehoshua Bin Nun street, something new accompanies me. I am entertaining the possibility, no, not entertaining the possibility—for this is not a thought, but rather a visceral sensation, a new knowing that we are all dwelling within a benign universe. I am surrounded by, and moving through this benevolence, a sensation which is so foreign it is almost indescribable, as though my very self is being reconstituted, a gentle revolutionary reordering taking place within me.

There are other changes as well. I had avoided being alone whenever possible, as aloneness aroused anxiety in me. These days I come home straight after work, shut the door behind me and unplug the phone. I enter my one room fifth floor walkup apartment as though it is a haven of tranquility and sacred space. Making dinner, cleaning up afterwards, reading, studying, just sitting—my mind is still enough to relish this doing and being, still enough to find a moment's peace.

It is during one such late afternoon, early evening, after I have returned from work, that I am sitting in the armchair next to the couch. My heart reflects on the love I feel for small and beautiful beings like babies and toddlers with dimpled wrists, for fuchsia lily pads floating on ponds, and furry newborn puppies with squinting eyes, tumbling over one another. Who even thought and reflected upon such things before? Unbidden, not part of a logical progression but rather as a rising awareness, it comes to me that I also am one more life form on this planet, the same as these tender, helpless beings. Precious just for being here and deserving also of love.

Why, in the quiet of my mind does the Sermon on the Mount call to me? I approach it warily; the image of Jesus on the Cross has always aroused discomfiting fear of the hatred and persecution of the Jews. What could possibly be waiting for me within the bindings of the New Testament? I ride the bus to Ramat Aviv and find the religion section in the University of Tel Aviv library. I am uneasy holding the Christian Bible in my hands and place the book down flat on the table hiding the words "New Testament" from any passerby who might glance my way. By reading these Scriptures am I betraying my people, am I turning away from our suffering? I read: "Blessed are the pure in heart for they will see God" and "Ask and it shall be given you, seek and you shall find, knock and it shall be opened unto you." The words "Many are called but few are chosen" echo in my thoughts. I do not know who said them or what they mean, yet sense there is a message in them for me.

I find the poems of Walt Whitman among the stacks in the American Literature section. Here I feel at home, and for a moment, it seems I will exit the library and emerge, not into the blinding sunlight of the Levant, but onto a leafy street of elm and maple trees in Ann Arbor. "I am large," I read, "I contain multitudes," and "For every atom belonging to me as good belongs to you." These words are the only touchstones I can think of to meet what is stirring within me.

My Israeli friends are concerned. This talk of a benign Universe, this mystical orientation possibly pointing to a notion of God— their only point of reference is another friend who recently became religious and then suffered a complete psychotic break. After Auschwitz, they say, what is there to believe?

My nascent, tiny, budding, opening into something for which I do not even have a name is no match for the constant undercurrent of danger in the ethers surrounding me, the daily threat of, say, a briefcase lying on the ground, or a discarded refrigerator on the curb calling forth the bomb sappers. Or the disquiet and unease of being required to spend a weekend locked in my apartment because a bus had been attacked several miles up the coastal road, thirty-eight people killed, seventy-one wounded. One of the terrorists, who arrived on dinghies from the sea, may have escaped the gun battle, may still be at large. Finally there is the claustrophobia of living on a tiny strip of land surrounded by enemies who never waver from their intention to push every single one of us into the sea.

What had not entered my thoughts even days earlier suddenly came forth as a full-blown decision: after a seven-year sojourn, it is time for me to leave Israel and return to the United States. A silver thread extending from the core of my body is leading me home.

Seventeen months later, I am sitting in my psychology graduate program classroom in Detroit. It is a cold, drab, barely endurable winter's day. For this gray wasteland I left the sparkling Mediterranean Sea, my White City of Tel Aviv? I feel I have gone from brilliant Technicolor to spirit-dulling black and white.

In class, we are exploring various spiritual traditions. Two people from an ashram in Ann Arbor have come to speak to us about their teacher and guru, Muktananda. "Ashram," "Muktananda"—I hear the words waking me from my regretful reverie. Where and when had I heard them spoken before? They use the word "shaktipat," which, they say, refers to the power of the guru to transmit spiritual illumination to a person simply by touching him or her. One can also receive shaktipat, they say, just by being in a room where the guru has been.

I begin to tremble as I listen, as though my body's dense form is wavering and morphing into currents of energy, as though I am being personally addressed by unseen guides. Was this what happened to me when I slept in Muktananda's bedroom, on his mattress? Had I received shaktipat? Was shaktipat the cause of the revolution in my life since the visit to California? Was all this a purposeful unfolding of my life's journey? Had a higher awareness awakened in me? Was it guiding my life in the direction of my soul's purpose?

I did not seek Muktananda, yet he found me.

The dueling forces of light and darkness within me were far from over, yet Muktananda's shaktipat had created an opening for a new light to come through.

PART 3

The Painting

CHAPTER 10

Hard Bed:

AN ACCOUNT OF A MARRIAGE
IN THREE PARTS

I made a hard bed for myself to lie on and
then I had to lie on it.

ERHAPS IRV'S MATTRESS, WHICH BECAME our marriage bed, should have been a clue. It had no give to it at all, only a hard surface resting on a frame of wooden planks.

"WHAT WILL BECOME OF DIANA?"

The evening I met Irv at the annual Christmas Eve Jewish Community Center Single's dance I was on a mission. And I would not hearken to any intuitive voice which might interfere with it. Now, in my mid-thirties, I was looking for, one could even say I was hellbent on finding, a life partner who wanted to marry and start a family.

Irv was handsome and might have been deemed strikingly so had he not been cut down to size by his short, almost stubby legs. Was I taken in by his handsome appearance, the seeming innocence and touch of whimsy of his blue denim shirt, blue jeans, and Betty Boop tie? His charm was not roguish, seductive, or conquering. I did not feel personally selected, but rather found myself in the purview of a kind of vivacious, momentary gaiety.

I wanted a happy ending to my story and was willing to cast a blind eye. But the signs were there, for within the hour of our meeting, after we had ascertained our common interests; our affinity for the Jewish people, for Israel, for literature, and a mutual longing for transcendent meaning in our lives, the encounter suddenly took on a grim and comfortless tone. A tense, cerebral, almost adversarial exchange ensued, involving a test of my Israeli political leanings and his combative conservative bent. I wondered how we had suddenly arrived, contrary to my intentions, expectations, or desire, to this darker place. The moment passed, but it seemed somehow to have been obligatory, as though a facedown of sorts was needed, something to cool off the sweetness and promise of the moments which had gone before.

I found all the outward reasons, and there were many, for why he was a good match for me, the answer to my prayers and longings, and I allowed myself to overlook or be talked out of whatever did not fit the "happy ending" picture I painted.

One afternoon, in the beginning of our courtship, we were lounging on the charcoal gray wool couch with its rounded curves, in the living room of his apartment. The room was barren of decoration and sparsely furnished, save for the couch and a burgundy, custom-made cabinet, expensive and ponderous. A sense of cool neglect pervaded the room's light. As I lay with upturned face on Irv's lap, I was not met with the gaze one would expect of a smitten and courting lover: dreamy infatuation, if not love, pouring from his eyes. Rather, his cold and critical eye, detached and unfeeling, regarded me, sending a chill up the front of my body.

"You have a wrinkle by your mouth," he said.

I lay there as though nothing untoward was happening, scrambling to dismiss the dismay in my heart.

I could not shake my unease though, and several days later, I related the incident to my psycho-spiritual advisor, Bert.

"You're too sensitive," he said. "Let's look at how you are using this incident with Irv to avoid relationship."

His assessment of my motives was what I wanted to believe, but wildly inaccurate. In truth, I was not avoiding attachment, rather I was slavishly and utterly dependent on a man to come along and bring with him the possibility of children, a warm hearth, and a good roof over my head. I needed a husband to give me a life—not because I did not have one—but because I did not value the one I had. It was as though I stood in a mere way station, a holding pattern, as I waited for the man and, thus, my true life to begin.

Thirty-five years old, my fantasy of the good life was caught between the women's movement which I ascribed to wholeheartedly in principle, and the Fifties, which still had a determining role in my psyche. Groomed to be a Mrs., being pretty and intelligent were necessary and sufficient. It was a given that he would cherish and be good to me, even dote on me. It was never mentioned or alluded to, nor had I seen in my mother's stance towards my father, that I might be expected to and would actually want to extend kindness and cherish him in return. And that doing so would bring me pleasure and joy. I should have known. How could I not have seen the most salient ingredient? But it simply never occurred to me.

One year before I met Irv, driving along in my car, I noticed a "For Sale" sign on a street with old trees, houses snuggled back barely visible from the road. I had not considered purchasing a home by myself, but this one rested on a magical little property with a small stream running through it, a rickety bridge matching the rickety little house, adding to its charm.

I brought my parents by to have a look. My father shook his head as we walked around the property. Back in the car, we were barely settled in our seats when the chorus began, voices of vehement opposition.

"A woman on her own, owning a house by herself?

The house is old, what will you do if something breaks down? You don't know how to fix anything. How will you take care of so much grass and land? Forget about a house and put your efforts into finding a good, Jewish husband."

Obsessive fretting about Diana, a habit begun when I lived in Israel, was my parents' evening pastime. They would sit together on the couch in the den, my father balancing his tea glass in one hand and in the other a tin of diabetic chocolate pieces, his one allowable treat.

"Where does she get these ideas?"

While I strayed out onto the pasture of my imagined future, my parents worried and sought to safely corral me into the pen with the rest. They were not charmed or amused by my eccentricities; the walks in nature alone with my books in my backpack, my spiritual path, the trips to retreat centers. My male friends: not lovers, not husbands, what are they? All well and good, but "*tachlis*," let's get to the point here, what was to become of their daughter? They sought a way to talk sense into me, to prevail upon me with reason. They lost sleep over it.

Truth be told, I had never in my life mowed the grass, turned over a flower bed, pulled weeds, or shoveled the snow. Nor could I rely on a steady income in my private psychotherapy practice. What was I thinking? My fantasies could get me into real trouble. I was relieved to back away. Still a deep yearning called, and I felt the loss and absence of its fulfillment; to be free to choose, to fashion my life from what lived within me. I longed to be like my friend Kathleen, with her wide feet and strong legs, whose alacrity with a heavy load I envied, her gazelle-like leap over a stream, her confidence and skill building a fire and setting up a tent.

As a pre-teen I was offered a babysitting job.

'How much will they pay you?" my father asked.

"Fifty cents an hour."

"Why should you change dirty diapers? Stay home and I will give you the money," he said.

The film "My Brilliant Career" was showing in a local art theater. My parents, who had seen the film, were cagey. They said they liked it but tried to talk me out of going. The movie "is not for you," they said. The main character had the opportunity to be lifted out of her straitened circumstances by a handsome, well-off suitor. She dreamt of being a writer and declined the marriage proposal in favor of the writing life. The film fades to black as we see her writing by lamplight in a gritty farmhouse.

In Israel, I had seen, accomplished, learned, and overcome so much during my years there:

- Learned to drive a stick shift, and in my little yellow Fiat, cruised up and down the length of the country
- Became fluent in Hebrew
- Awakened to sexual fulfillment
- Completed a degree in Clinical Social Work at Tel Aviv University
- Worked for the Municipality of Tel Aviv with street gangs and prostitutes
- Worked in community mental health in Jaffa
- Received an award from Defense Minister Shimon Peres for my work with parents who lost their sons in the Yom Kippur War
- Made lifelong friendships
- Lived in a fifth floor, one room, walkup apartment without heat, air conditioning, a stove, or reliable hot water and managed just fine.

In the five years since my return, it was as though I had given all these accomplishments away, discounted them, and instead, took on my mother's view of me as having wasted my time, fallen behind my girlfriends who were married and living in nice homes and "knew what they wanted." The forcefield of this zero-sum game pervaded her thinking and mine. If my friends held the gains, then I held the losses, my gains utterly and totally erased by theirs.

Somehow, my mother was able to turn everything around so that I was neither adventurous, resourceful, nor courageous and had not been enriched either by the experience of living in a foreign country or since my return to the U.S., by obtaining another degree in Humanistic and Clinical Psychology. I was a disappointment and failure for I had not attained the only goal worth having—marriage to a well-established Jewish man.

And I believed her, not a simple belief one could refute with facts, rather a whole-body response of teary, trembling weakness.

On Mother's Day, I gave her a skirt, blouse, and jacket of lush fabric in the fuchsia, purple, and pink tones she loved. She was surprised and pleased by the rather extravagant gift. Perhaps the extravagance made her uncomfortable, for she said, "Why don't you buy yourself nice clothes? Why don't you dress nice?"

The worse offense I could commit was to make her look bad in the survivor community. Returning from a shiva call, she phoned to let me know that she saw Mrs. F. who mentioned she had seen me and was surprised at how old I looked.

"Why are you telling me this?" I asked.

"Because I felt so bad when she said it."

"So if you feel bad you must be sure that I will feel bad as well?"

"I only want you to look good."

I colluded in my own undoing. Was it my continuing struggle with anxiety and depression which allowed me to relinquish who I was? That and the losses and difficulty of starting over in America after years of being away, an America transformed into disco strangeness? Or was it the drip, drip, drip of my mother's negativity and judgments piled on top of the damage caused by the traumas, which left me hollowed out and insubstantial?

"You are intelligent and beautiful," she would say. Why hadn't I used those gifts and done the right thing with them? I had missed the boat, taken the wrong trip, traveled on a journey to nowhere. Although I fought and argued with her, my body soaked up the insinuations in her words.

"When will the sun shine on our side of the street?" was her refrain.

Her words resounded within me until I was vacant inside, wiped clean of organs and a backbone, reduced and diminished, barely able to stand. After a visit with her, I would crawl back to my apartment and take to my bed. I pulled the covers over my head thinking death would be better than this.

Bert's insistence on playing down the incident on the couch with Irv was what I secretly wanted to hear. His remarks gave me the green light to go ahead with the relationship, to look for the fault within myself, even for that heart-chilling moment, and to disregard and distrust my own gut knowing. I wonder now how it all would have unfolded had Bert responded simply by saying;

"That doesn't sound right. You deserve kindness and most of all, to feel safe." Would his words have made a difference?

After yoga class, Sheri said:

"Remember the time we traveled to Toronto, you, Irv, Dan, and me? Irv was vicious towards you from the moment we got into the car," she said.

"We went to Toronto?"

"Don't you remember? It was before he became religious, in the beginning years. Dan and I talked about how vicious he was towards you."

"I don't remember that at all."

I would not have known "he was vicious towards me," even if I had remembered. I would have been sick with shame because we "weren't getting along" and there were witnesses to our unhappiness. I would have felt dismay that yet again I was wrong and bad and someone who was meant to love me, did not like me. Feeling battered, I would have blamed myself for the assault.

An unease haunted me, one I was afraid to face or name. How did I bring these troubles upon myself? What did I bring to the table? Surely the constant flow of emotional over-reaction and drama in which I indulged was a heavy burden for my partner. And I had learned from an expert the craft of superiority, criticism, and blame. Worst of all, though I had been devalued and diminished, I had also been indulged—thus I leaned away from giving (feeling enervated at the thought) yet felt much was owed me.

Reading my journals from the years with Irv, beginning Christmas Eve, 1983—falling back into that time of my life, was like being engulfed in a bad, recurring dream I was loathe to revisit.

"What bothers me is that I wonder about the sincerity of Irv's emotions. Sometimes I feel he is exaggerating or falsifying them, conjuring up the appropriate emotional response to fit a situation or get a desired effect without having the feelings purported to be there. When this occurs, when I sense his faking, I feel very uneasy, uncomfortable, and the little girl within me feels despair. There is a part of Irv that is for show and plays to the crowd and tries to manipulate me. Which leads me to the next problem. I don't totally trust Irv. I often find myself wondering how he'll act five years from now. ... My suspicion is that his father in him will come out and he will be inconsiderate and selfish and maneuver to have me in his power."

Another journal entry from February 1990, some months before the end:

"Irv called me a shmuck today. He said, 'I will shred you to pieces.' He called me a pig who eats pig."

When he left, I never missed him, not even for a moment. When he left it was enough that he was gone, and I was free.

BACK TO THE SHTETL

Strong currents of freedom were moving across the globe. The seemingly impossible had happened—the Berlin Wall had fallen; Nelson Mandela was released from prison. While freedom was on the rise for many, I was losing mine one step at a time. The vise of the men in the black hats, the ultra-Orthodox Jews with whom Irv had cast his lot, was circling, tightening, around me. Oblivious to the incipient danger, I had not taken those men seriously when they materialized in my life. Of course, in the beginning, I had no frame of reference to imagine the power they could and would have over me.

The day we parted for the last time at the realtor's office, Irv wore a long black beard, a black hat and black suit, and the fringes of his four-cornered undergarment, the *tzitzit*, hung below his waist. This is the garb worn by the Jews of Europe in the eighteenth and nineteenth century, still worn today by the ultra-religious Jews whose community my husband Irv had joined. In parting, he refused to shake the outstretched hand of the female real estate agent who managed the sale of our home. He lifted his hands, palms forward in front of his face, half bowing in a "kindly" gesture of refusal, looking for all the world like an obsequious ghetto Jew. An ultra-Orthodox religious man is forbidden to touch a woman who is not his wife.

During our first year of marriage, Irv was invited to join a two-year study program for young Jewish community leaders. He savored every moment of the readings and classes, especially the religious teachings given by authors flown in for the evening lectures. When the program ended, Irv intended to continue his religious studies. He approached the rabbi of the congregation to which his family had a long affiliation and to which we now also belonged. The rabbi, however, was not amenable to taking on a student. He had a large and prosperous congregation to consider, his own little empire to attend, and he sent Irv on his way. This was a fateful turning, for Irv was then referred to a rabbi at the Kollel, a Yeshiva-like institute for advanced study of Jewish text, designed for married men. The Kollel rabbi was only too happy to take on Irv as a student and protégé.

And so it began, when, some weeks later, Irv announced he would be keeping the Sabbath this coming Friday night and Saturday, practicing Shabbat as it is meant to be observed. My father happened by that Saturday afternoon. Irv, barely able to contain his excitement, his eyes, even at that early stage, lit by a feverish glow, shared with my father this latest project and endeavor.

"Put a stop to this," my father said when Irv left the room. "Don't let this go any further. You don't know these religious people like I do; I know them from 'home.' They are fanatics."

The dreary clouds of the autumn afternoon, the dim, descending light lending a clandestine aura to the room where we stood, matched the low, urgent tone in which my father spoke to me. The joy of his spontaneous visit fading, we stood close, heads bowed towards one another. I was again failing to give him "*naches*," fulfillment in his children. The pleasure he might have felt seeing me in my clean, spacious home, living with my Jewish husband whom he had urged me to marry, was set aside with this new concern. My efforts to assure him of my happiness, the twirling wind-up doll self I often presented to him, did not convince. Instead, as I attempted to evade his worried look and the import of his words, he saw the tide rising and building, foresaw how it would inexorably wash over me.

My father, prescient in his seeing, could not know the impossibility of the task he put before me. To stem the tide of Irv's "return" in its inception would have required I have influence over him as another wife might have, a wife with a different kind of husband; a husband with the ability to love reliably, not someone intractable like Irv, whose *raison d'être* was to be a maverick who thrived in opposition, thrived when going against the grain.

I could not have stopped this sea change had I wanted to. In the first blush of its emergence, I welcomed it, as a way Irv might find some palliative to his anger—some peace. I was totally innocent and ignorant of the "black hats," unlike my father, who was familiar with their unyielding, backward-looking fanaticism.

From that day forward, I embarked on a return voyage to the Pale of Settlement, to the shtetl. I did not choose to leave the late 20th century behind, had no need or desire to go, did not even know I was leaving. Thousands, hundreds of thousands, almost two million Jews left the shtetls of Poland and Russia, fled the pogroms and Cossack raids, flocked onto ships praying to make it safely to America, the "Goldene Medina," the Golden Land—and I was voyaging in reverse, without even stepping on a packed boat, without going down into steerage, traveling backwards to shtetl life.

Friday evening at sunset was the start of the Sabbath. Irv began his preparations in the afternoon; leaving work early, rushing, shopping for groceries, buying flowers, cooking dinner. Not that he was spending much time at his office anymore. He woke early in the morning as before and left the house wearing his business suit. But instead of going to work, he would head to the Kollel, join the men for morning prayers. He was warmly received in their fellowship and would linger afterwards, share a light breakfast with them, and a schmooze. He then rolled into his office around ten o'clock or later. His business faltered. Our health insurance bills were overdue and sometimes left unpaid and he lost the large mainstay account which kept his business enterprise afloat. In the early evening after work, he returned to the Kollel for evening prayers, never returning home before eight o'clock.

He rushed around all Friday afternoon frantically preparing for the Sabbath. I did not roll up my sleeves and jump in to help. I did not purchase the groceries or get the dinner going, rather leaving it to him. It pains me now to remember the sweat on his face, the tension in his body, as he hurried and rushed. Grocery shopping, food, and cooking were difficult for me, stemming from problematic roots beginning in my infancy. It was Irv who taught me to cook, so that later I was able to prepare, invite, and host. But there was more to my lack of participation. I resented this way of life he was forcing upon me. I wanted to go out for the evening, to be free to have dinner in a restaurant with our friends, see a good film, stop for a coffee. It was enough to set the table beautifully, I told myself, to do all the cleanup.

The dining room in our home, with its open floor plan and light-colored Berber carpeting throughout, had two delicately framed Japanese prints on the wall. The windows were covered with panels of transparent white rice paper. The oak dining table with its spare, simple lines, the luminous Sabbath candles in their crystal holders—all lent an atmosphere of serenity and calm to the quiet house. I liked to imagine that perhaps after all, in spite of everything, in spite of all the coercion and resistance—the spirit of the Sabbath, the *Shechinah*, the holy presence, was gracing this home. I wanted to believe in the possibility.

Since I could no longer go out with my friends on Friday evening, I invited them to join us for dinner, even those who were not Jewish. The friends I recruited, loyal and kind, who joined me in my exile, were waiting with me when Irv came in from the synagogue after the evening service.

He found his place at the head of the table and the time-honored rituals began. First the singing of the Kiddush, followed by the blessings over the bread and wine. It is coming back to me now—how heavy handed it felt as he tore the challah the way he had watched other heads of household do, his arched wrist covered with black hairs, the arc of the saltshaker throwing salt indiscriminately around the environs of his plate and on the pieces of challah, passing the challah around. My guests and I could only observe, they because they were ignorant of the language and customs, I because I was female.

The singing of the Kiddush—it is almost unimaginable this could be a defining moment in a marriage, could drag the entire edifice crashing down.

As a child of eight or nine, the Kiddush, the chanting, was mine. My father gave it to me at the Passover Seder. I was to lead, to sing the prayer in Hebrew. I did it for him, to make up for the loss of his family, to make him smile with my ardor. And he did smile, my father, delighted and proud, he called me "the little Rebbetzin" with such fondness.

Now Irv was taking it from me, at the same time he was shoving it down my throat. Perhaps I could join in the singing, I thought. Rather than sitting in passive resistance, rather than wishing it to be over and cringing at Irv's adopted mannerisms and Yiddish inflections, I could become involved. "Be well," he had begun to say, like the Yiddish "*zie gezundt*," or "I am going by David's house" instead of "to." The irony of Irv—whose family took such pride in their longevity in America, who considered themselves aristocrats in the Jewish hierarchy—turning himself into an old country Jew, was not lost on me.

Bastardizing the warmth of Yiddish onto his stiff inflexibility, he forsook all others in his devotion to this new-found identity, as he had grafted on other identities before this one. He usurped my childhood in the immigrant community of survivors with their Yiddish jokes and accents as though he was the authentic one, and then gave it back to me altered into something unrecognizable, devoid of juiciness, absent the intrinsic joy and humor of its essence.

Even his name was a graft. He eschewed "Ian," the name given to him by his parents at birth, the name he carried for his first thirty years, and he became Irving; choosing his grandfather's name. Later, he officially became Yitzhak, I heard, another name change in his lifelong search for a virtuous identity. Perhaps he finally found one; I don't know. I can't say.

My proposal was to sing the Kiddush together, Irv and me. This was the vision I brought to him, my heart in my hands. How to come to terms with the life he had thrust upon me? I was no longer an actor and co-creator of our family life, only a reluctant observer and tagalong. I sought a creative way to find a stance between resistance and submission, a platform of personal expression. I could not allow Irv and the rabbis to return to me the image of God as a harsh judge and smiter. The benign Universe I had reached towards must not be disappeared by the black hatters who pulled in the wrathful God of the Old Testament.

Irv said he would consult with the rabbis on the matter of my request. Several days later, he turned on me in fury. This was the last straw, he said, this intention of mine to usurp his role as the man, to compete with him, to debase him as head of the household, to seek to sing the Kiddush together.

I do not intend to infer here that Irv's newfound Orthodoxy was hypocritical or insincere, for truly it was sincere, the answer to his prayers, a perfect fit. He struggled with psycho-sexual aberrations and impulses (revealed to me one week before our wedding). Strict religious enforcement of the ultra-Orthodox practice of Judaism would protect him from these urges, help him to master them and keep them in check. He found what his parched soul deeply needed and longed for—a blueprint for living —everything spelled out, mapped out. Follow this road and you are assured of being a worthy and good man. In his new community they called him a "Tzaddik," a righteous one. This was balm for the pain of the wounds inflicted by his tyrannical father—these male mentors and authority figures raining approval and kindness upon him. And his choice of Ultra-Orthodoxy was a good match for the deep thirst of his intellect: if he lived to be one hundred he would only arrive at a beginning knowledge of the rich teachings of the Torah, the Talmud, and the Mishnah.

He found the perfect path for him, and I did not and do not begrudge him this. Total immersion was his way, and the love he had for me, whatever it had been, was not a match, and could not stand contra to this powerful, newfound force. I became a deterrent, an irritant, "a ball and chain around his leg," as he wrote on a piece of paper left on the couch in his study.

During dinner, our guests and I sat and listened to Irv. Table talk was restricted by Irv to topics in the spirit of the Torah, the five books of Moses—the only fitting conversation for Sabbath eve. Mostly it was he who spoke, who waxed eloquent about the wondrousness of his new path, the purity of his newfound purpose, the joy gained by following the Law. He elucidated, in his new singsong delivery, the meaning and sanctity of unscrewing the light bulb in the refrigerator before the start of the Sabbath and the necessity before the Sabbath of tearing toilet paper into sections. These acts would allow strict observance of the Sabbath during which tearing and igniting electricity were prohibited, as they are regarded as acts of changing something in Creation. My dear friends sat listening respectfully, asked questions, and surreptitiously looked my way with pitying glances.

When the third star was seen in the sky, signifying the end of the Sabbath on Saturday evening, and the Havdalah ritual had been performed, signifying a return to the mundane from the holy, my husband was free to use electricity, to shave and to shower so that we could join our friends for an evening out. Unfortunately, as our evening was beginning, theirs was already winding down, the late hour a deterrent, but not the only one. Strict observance of the laws of kashrut eventually made it impossible for my husband to take anything to mouth in restaurants or at the homes of friends and family.

I had my own understanding of why this entire protocol founded by the ancient rabbis was constructed. Beginning with the fall of the Temple and the dispersal of the Jews by the Romans, the need arose to dictate every aspect of life in order to maintain Jewish identity. By separating the Jewish community from the community of nations whom the Jews were now forced to live among, assimilation could be averted. If we could not break bread outside the group, if we could not participate in the surrounding culture, if our children must learn Torah and therefore must be taught in separate schools, if we dressed differently and spoke a different language, there would be no chance of "contamination" by the dominant culture.

Unable to maintain our former active social life, a drift towards the families of Irv's new community seemed the natural next step. Thus, I crossed over the threshold into the world of the shtetl, newly resurrected here in America. Ordinarily, I would be interested and eager to meet new people and learn about their ways. Spending a Shabbat evening or holiday in the home of an ultra-Orthodox family would have intrigued me. But this was not an anthropological field study of a quaint lifestyle. This was my husband transformed into one of them, insisting this would be our life, the world we must now inhabit.

I entered homes reflecting the virtues of modesty and simplicity, homes absent of decoration, save the silver candelabra embracing the holy candle lights of Shabbos and the framed photographs of the rebbes. I was introduced to the many children, tiny to grown, with names like Yosele, Rivkale, Sarale, Avramele, Moishele, and Rochele. The wives wore long-sleeved matronly dresses down to their ankles and wigs covering their shorn heads. They prepared generous tables laden with heavy Eastern European food, as they cared for five, six, or seven children, all under the age of ten. The husbands, sitting at the head of the table waiting to be served, pulled heavy tomes of Jewish learning from the bookshelves lining the walls of the room, in order to illustrate a point of Torah. The male children were asked to speak about the weekly Torah portion, testing their studiousness and knowledge.

It was a mitzvah, a good deed, to invite guests for the Sabbath meal and an even greater mitzvah and honor to bring a new initiate, a "*baal tshuva,*" one who has come back to the faith, into one's home.

They must have heard about poor Irv's recalcitrant, difficult wife who wanted no part of the "return," but they were kind and unfailingly polite towards me, most probably hoping their influence would eventually open my eyes to the only right and holy way for a Jew to live.

I treated them with respect and friendliness in return, except the one time when I acted shamefully, and had to leave the Sabbath lunch table and walk home by myself. Or perhaps, looking back, it was they who acted shamefully, fanatically, and cruelly. It began as all the other times. We sat around the table with its white tablecloth; the Kiddush had been sung; the wine had been blessed. Now it was time to walk over to the kitchen sink and wash our hands using a two-handled pitcher to pour right and left, say the blessing, and not speak a word until the challah was torn, salted, passed around, and a bite taken, chewed, and swallowed.

Perhaps there was something about this particular family we were visiting for the first time, something sour and dour and lifeless. I just could not carry on, could not participate; my gorge was rising in my throat. I could not bear all this forced upon me yet again, one more time, one more day. When the others went to wash their hands, I remained in my seat. No one commented, no one said a word, eyes were cast down. When the father passed the pieces of challah around the table, he bypassed me, as though I were air. I was not allowed to receive bread. By the time the chicken soup was brought to the table and served, my throat was tight, burning with shame and anger and I could barely imbibe a few spoonfuls. Abruptly, I stood and walked out of the house, crying all the way home. This was my one moment of open, public rebellion, or, you could say, childish acting out, during the five years of countless Shabbat lunches and dinners, weddings, and lectures, the latter where the women and men were required to sit apart, separated by an aisle or in the case of a wedding, by a partition.

"I respect your spiritual path." I said to Irv as we sat in the dining room, the table strewn with leftovers from a Sabbath meal. "I see how fulfilling it is for you."

We were relaxing together in a friendly way.

"The way I see it," I said, "or one way to think of it is this—imagine that the sun is God, the Divine, and the sun's rays are pathways one can ride up to God. All religions and spiritual paths are vehicles people use to ride up to the Holy. Each ray when traveled with pure intention is as legitimate as any other."

His eyes were on mine as he listened, and I went on:

"Judaism is a beautiful path which speaks to your heart, it is your vehicle, your ray up to God, but it is not the Only Way or even the True Way, it is one way." I was stepping into dangerous territory here, but he did not blow up or even argue.

I hoped this talk would bring an easing and open a space for moderation and compromise, but it was not to be. At the same time, a nagging fear plagued me; what if I am wrong? What if they are right? Five thousand years of Jewish history, of adherence to the teachings, of brilliant sages devoting their lives to the study of the holy texts. Who am I to question everything? Should I be following this path? Is it the true path? What right do I have to doubt it? Who am I to think in terms of historical context, in terms of tribal cultures? The Torah was written by God and it is held in utter and total reverence. How dare I reduce it to a compilation of narratives and myths written by different scholars in different time periods? I had moments of primitive, superstitious terror—have I made God angry?

SURVIVING THE PATRIARCHY

It seemed I had no sooner made the necessary accommodations, having barely adjusted to a new rule or stricture, when Irv would up the ante and bring in another law to be observed, one even more onerous.

Thus I was introduced to the laws of family purity. The holy tradition decreed that as soon as the wife's menses began, the husband was forbidden to touch her, not even pinky finger to pinky finger. When her menstrual flow ceased entirely, five to seven days after it began, she was obliged to insert a small white linen cloth into her vagina to be certain there is no more blood, a rabbi available to ascertain the meaning of any suspicious brown spot found on the white fabric. The wife must then count seven more days and then is required to go to the ritual bath, the mikveh, to be cleansed. She is inspected by the mikveh attendant from head to toe for cleanliness. Then she is watched as she immerses herself fully underwater three times and says the proper blessing. Upon returning home from the mikveh, conjugal relations must resume.

The day came to pass when Irv informed me from now on he would treat me "kindly and affectionately" but would not touch me unless I agreed to go to the mikveh and follow the laws of family purity to the letter. This latest was an assault on the very lived sensation of my skin, the delicate tissue of my nether parts, my inner sanctum, my vulnerable, tender me. Even here the men in the black hats, the patriarchal owners of female bodies, sought to enter.

A journal excerpt written before we were married:

> "I noticed at the party Friday night that Irv wanted to snuff out my light, wanted to kill it. I felt his jealousy of my spontaneity and openness, his jealousy of my receiving love and attention from my friends. I felt him trying to hurt me and control me and I felt how my pleasure was diminished. Irv admitted this aspect of himself, he has owned that he fears this in himself; he does want to crush me and destroy me. And he says he wants to go to therapy and work on it."

This was right up my alley, relationship as one long psychotherapy process. Pick a partner who is willing to "do the work," "be in process" and everything will work out fine. I did not require a baseline sense of safety with my partner, such a sense did not live within me. I did not have an inner template. Comfort and welfare while in the presence of another were abstract concepts I barely knew and did not expect to feel. Save for the brief interlude with Yonatan, I never had. Unease and being devalued were as familiar to me as the face I saw in the mirror each morning, as the air I breathed. I just needed to find someone who "wanted to work on himself" so that in some far-off future, things would be different. Irv wanted to expand his emotional range and bare his soul to me, he had said. He would do anything it took to be a good husband.

Now he denies controlling me; he is not controlling or mean, he says. It is simply a woman's duty to follow her husband. He is taking me down a path of righteousness, to the true faith, to Judaism as it is meant to be lived, as it is decreed in the holy books compiled over thousands of years of rectitude, a path which is pleasing to God.

"And," he said, "you will see. If you follow the laws of family purity we will be given a child."

Since Wednesday night when Rosh Hashanah began up to to-day, Saturday—Shabbat, Irv has walked to and from synagogue services six times. The blue skies, the warm sun, the canopy of colorful autumn leaves overhead and the sound of their crispness underfoot, enhance his reverie of blessedness. These walks are a balm to his soul, a chance to reflect on the goodness the path he has chosen has brought him. He takes a handkerchief and wipes away the sweat dripping down from under the hat band of his black hat. The drip of perspiration trickling down his back underneath his dark wool suit is his sensual immersion into this life of Biblical injunction.

After performing the required prayers and rituals and eating our Sabbath afternoon meal, I clean the kitchen while Irv goes into the bathroom, takes a wet cold cloth, and wipes down his hirsute body. He cannot bathe or use hot water since heating water is forbidden on the holidays and Sabbath. But lovemaking on Shabbat is a mitzvah and what better time than after the Sabbath meal and before a nice long nap.

He invites me into our bedroom, to our bed, and pulls my body towards his. I welcome his embrace, long for the closeness and warmth of being together, even as my senses recoil from the appearance of his greasy, matted down hair, the oiliness of his musty skin and the odor of sweat emanating from his body. With Irv's arousal comes his involuntary burping reflex and his mouth close to mine brings odors as well. As I am aroused by his caresses, my pleasure heightening, he suddenly and inadvertently lands awkwardly on my knee cap. A yelp of pain escapes me before I can blunt it. Quickly covering over the moment, fearing Irv will turn away in anger at my "overreaction," I seek to refocus and regain my arousal. This epitomizes my struggle during those years. In order to be connected to Irv, I needed to disregard myself, even down to the most fundamental level of my lived experience.

But now even this conflicted intimacy had ended— as dictated by the laws of family purity. For several months, he was "kind" but did not touch me. The pause in our sexual relations did not seem to trouble him. I wondered whether he experienced abstinence as a sacrifice at all. Perhaps it was a relief. When I brought my passion to him, he would giggle and pull back. Even before this, he had taken to withholding his thrusts just when I began to climax, as if he would be swallowed up by my convulsions of pleasure, as though he must control even this.

I balked for several months and then I folded and gave myself over to the ministrations of the mikveh attendant in a building within walking distance of my home. Who knew, just a few short years earlier, that such a place even existed?

Irv's prediction came to pass as he said it would. We were given a child. Coincidence? A gift from God for following His Laws?

Several months after agreeing to abide by the laws of family purity, I received a phone call from California. The attorney's office to which we sent photo albums depicting our lives, including our bios, and an open letter to the birthmother, phoned to inform us we had been chosen by a birthmother, six months pregnant, to be the prospective parents of the male child in her womb. Driving to the supermarket later that rainy evening, crying ecstatic tears of wonder and joy, I named it: "The curse is lifted, the curse of childlessness is lifted."

Years of sorrowful infertility had brought intensified pressure to bear on our difficult union, Irv's and mine. Childlessness had become the proof of our flawed natures. We were both trying in so many ways to fix ourselves, to lighten the darkness we carried within us. I tried to fix myself through psychotherapy and my spiritual path. Irv turned to an extreme form of religion. But were we so different on the level of causality, in the motivation behind our efforts?

I wanted a child with all my heart. During my long walks, I would talk to Spirit, reach towards the Divine. One day in particular, my vision of a child was powerful within me. I made a sacred vow: "Please give me a child and I will give my best. I will give more than my best; I promise, and I swear."

And later, when I was called upon to give much more than I thought my best could or ever would be, I gave without question, gave everything I had.

I would do it all over again too —and give even better this time because I understand so much more.

On a Sunday morning, when our son was fifteen months old, my husband returned from synagogue in the afternoon, having been gone, as usual, since early morning.

"You never help with the baby, you're never home."

"The best thing I can do for my son is study Torah."

"But a child needs to see his father."

He gets up close to my face, dark eyes pouring hatred, shouting. "Fuck you, Fuck you, Fuck you!"

Irv's screaming wakes the baby who, startled, begins to cry. I run to his room where he stands in his crib, his little dimpled hands clutching the guard rail.

Irv's newfound, kindly countenance and comportment is known to his prayer buddies at the Kollel, but they should only see him now—red faced, mouth foaming, and shouting obscenities.

"I want a divorce," I said.

Some months earlier—a Friday before sunset, the Sabbath bearing down with the lateness of the hour, the baby crawling on the floor underfoot; my mother was visiting as Irv and I were putting groceries away and preparing dinner. Something set Irv off, perhaps a request from my mother at a moment when he was hurrying and rushing. Suddenly he exploded, grabbing dishes from the cupboard, and throwing them on the floor. I watched in horror as shards of dishes bounced and flew in every direction, missing the baby's eyes by inches.

"Stop, stop!" I screamed, my mother's wordless cries joining mine. She and I stood in unbelieving shock for several seconds and then I scooped the baby into my arms and my mom and I ran out of the kitchen towards the bedroom.

Holding the baby in my arms, my mother and I sat trembling, shaking—

"Oh my God, oh my God," we said.

The next day my mother suffered a massive heart attack.

Later that Sunday evening, we stood in my white-tiled bathroom adjoining our bedroom. Irv's bathroom, the one off the hall, had been relegated to him six years earlier by me when we moved into the house, and was another source of resentment he felt towards me. Wearing his magenta and rose-colored robe which flattered his olive skin and dark black hair, my white nightgown bright in the light, our reflections were mirrored in the long horizontal mirror over the sink.

"Are you sure you meant what you said?" he asked. "Do you really want a divorce?"

"I can't allow you to abuse me anymore. I'm done," was my reply.

Was he asking me to reconsider? Why was he not jumping at the chance to get rid of me? Did this mean he cared for me a little?

If there was ever a time in my entire life when a course of wise action needed to be contemplated, when I needed to look three steps ahead on the chessboard before I made a move, this was the time. Any moment but this one to plunge ahead with my usual *modus vivendi*—"be your authentic self, be direct, speak and act from the heart and all will be well." Had I been using strategic thinking, I would have abjured all that had been said earlier in the day about divorce and bided my time, would have waited patiently until our son's adoption was finalized in court six weeks hence.

"I want a divorce, I said." "I will not live like this anymore."

I drew a line in the sand. Somehow, without my knowing it, this act of claiming my life released a greater wisdom. Unseen forces responded to my rash claim and engineered events in a totally unexpected way; a mystical interference I never could have conjured up on my own. Our human emotions and foibles play out on the stage, while an unseen hand guides the outcome.

Irv consulted his mentors and put an ultimatum before me. Either I sign a legal document committing to full agreement to raise my son in the strictest observance of my husband's tradition—he would have him for every Jewish holiday and every Sabbath, my son would attend a Yeshiva school, my home would follow the laws of Kashrut to the letter—or Irv would sue me in court for full custody. I consulted with attorneys who said I must sign the document in order not to jeopardize the finalization of the adoption.

"Now you will have all the difficulties of abiding by the religion with none of the perks," Irv said.

He watched my every move. I dared not carry our son out of the house on the Sabbath (carrying is not allowed), nor give him any food to eat at my parents' home or friends' homes or a restaurant, God forbid. I carried a small pink cooler filled with Raphie's food and his little spoon whenever we left the house. On the Sabbath, Irv took the baby away to the homes of people in his community, leaving the little fifteen-month-old baby to sit on the living room floor with the other children, while Irv spent the morning and evening at the synagogue.

Can a heart really break, can it crack into tiny pieces, burst with pain, explode? I felt mine would.

A month later a Solomonic dilemma arose.

The Beit Din, the rabbinical court whose word is law in the Ultra-Orthodox community issued its edict. Our son, who was not born of a Jewish mother, had been in the process of conversion to Judaism. Step one, the Bris, the circumcision, was held in our home shortly after his birth. It is a mitzvah to attend a Bris and Irv's community turned out in full force. The police were called to bring order to the traffic situation in the adjacent streets. The baby, laying on a pillow on my father's lap as the mohel performed the circumcision, was surrounded by a sea of black hats, the mass of the men's bodies blocking the view of the proceedings from all of our invited guests.

The second step in the conversion process, the dunking in the mikveh and the blessings recited from which one emerged a full-fledged Jew, had not yet taken place.

During the previous several days I thought I noticed an easing of Irv's intense scrutiny regarding my actions with the baby. This easing, though welcome, confused and concerned me.

On Sunday afternoon, Irv said he needed to speak with me.

"You are not an Observant Jew." he said. "Since we are going for joint custody of Raphael and he will be living with you part of the time, the Rabbinical Court has decreed they cannot sanction the completion of Raphael's conversion to Judaism. Of course, I cannot be the father of a child who is not a Jew."

"Wait, what are you saying? I signed the agreement, I agreed to everything."

"The court decided it is in the best interest of the child that only one of us becomes his parent. Otherwise the child will be torn between two worlds. Only one of us can have him…. You can't live without him, and I can, so you can have him."

Thus Irv was airbrushed out of the photo of the three of us: the photo of me sporting a toothy, wide grin ("yay, hooray, I have a husband and a baby now") and Irv smiling, his head leaning into mine protectively. The baby is sitting on my lap, wearing a yellow shirt, denim overalls and blue sneakers with little yellow boats on them. His small face is wearing a look of concern, as if he could see what was ahead and was wondering what might become of him.

There was a note on the counter from Irv in the eating nook in the kitchen, and something about its tone and content, the disinterested separateness of him, brought the truth home to me, slamming it into my chest. He doesn't care about us. I could not absorb this standing still. Setting Raphie into the child seat on the back, I climbed on my bike and rode through random streets, pedaling and sobbing wildly—when my attention was drawn to a gentle tap, tap, tapping against the small of my back. Raphie's little head in its helmet was bobbing against me as the drowsy gliding of the bike on the pavement brought his chin down to his chest and lulled him to sleep. It is just the two of us now, I thought, this precious small being is utterly dependent on me. My shaky legs will have to bear the weight and grow strong in the vigor of it, carrying both of us. Love would need to be the fulcrum which would propel me into emotional and financial independence, into becoming what I longed to become, a woman of substance.

The matter of custody was now turned over to the civil courts. I had escaped the clutches of Irv and the rabbis, only to find a greater danger lurking.

"You must steel yourself," the attorney said.

"Once the court finds out Irv refuses to go through with the adoption, they might very well take the baby back into their custody and give him to a family with two parents."

The social worker on the case spoke with Irv, begging him to go through with the adoption, and then later to rescind his parental rights, but he wouldn't hear of it.

"I don't want any outstanding financial responsibility." he told her.

"Please Irv, please," I said. "You can renege on your parental rights later. Please go through with the adoption. If you don't and they take Raphie away, it will kill my parents."

"You are the one who brought this upon them. A woman should follow her husband."

Waiting for the court's decision, I returned to the vigil of terror I experienced the night my father was shot. Once again, my body shook in a cold sweat, as though vibrating on terror alert, heart pounding, thoughts racing to panic, while I ran to the bathroom again and again, my entire system a twisted knot of uncontrollable agitation reacting to the possibility of a loss which threatened to overwhelm me.

Sometime in the middle of the night, from my sleeplessness and barely endurable fear, the darkness threatening to engulf me, I cried out to God and the angels, to every kind spirit or Realized Being, and at last to Etty Hillesum, whose journals were published several years earlier as *An Interrupted Life* —

"Etty, oh Etty, please help me, dear Spirit sister, sweet taliswoman. While I opened to Spirit under the shadow of the Holocaust in a garden in California, on Yehoshua Bin Nun street in Tel Aviv, daring to poke my consciousness out like a tiny green shoot reaching towards the sun; you awakened to Spirit in the streets of occupied Amsterdam, in the camp at Westerbork, where Nazis weren't phantoms of terror in your dreams, but menacing real men wearing black polished boots, strutting on sidewalks, their growling dogs pulling on leashes as they herded you onto the train to Auschwitz. I call out to you in the night from my terror, dear Etty. In the midst of hell, you realized a transcendent function—in hell your awakened consciousness expanded and embraced. Before "knowing" you, the Holocaust loomed overpoweringly large, always holding my new consciousness in doubt, wondering if I would have withstood the "biggest test." It is your awakening I can trust and turn to in my hour of need, you I can ask to help me find courage and strength."

Etty's spirit comforted as no other could. Her presence reassured, slowed my heart rate, warmed, and dried my cold, clammy body and blessedly allowed me to sink into a few hours of sleep.

In the end, the social worker and then the judge recognized the strong bond between Raphie and me and "for the good of the child" it was decided we would not be separated.

Like the haunted people of Romania, who even after the execution of their dictator Ceausescu, remained intimidated and fearful, I continued to look over my shoulder in nervous wariness, skittish of being berated for one transgression or another. The process of losing oneself to tyranny reverses and unwinds slowly, returning the self to the self gradually over time. The disappearance of oppressive restrictions, the sheer pleasure of their absence, helped offset minefields of fearful thoughts concerning the responsibility of raising a son without a father. I lay in bed, Raphie's warm body heavy with sleep beside me, delicious peace and rightness descending, chains melting away, as I watched on television the sun shining down on the crowd, Paul Simon on stage singing "Graceland" in Africa. This is my world, I thought, this community of rainbow colors and freedom seekers. I have returned to it with a sweet embrace.

Ever so slowly, setting one toe and then an entire foot outside the front door on a Saturday with Raphie in my arms, I crossed the threshold. I was free to go where I wished.

Had Irv truly been kind, had he integrated love for me with love of God, had he not used religious observance as a means of control and abuse, would I have remained in his world? His world of Tradition was determined by fixed and rigid rules and roles, by ethnocentricity, by social conservatism, and God as a harsh judge. Irv's life was subsumed under an "ism" and the danger with "isms" is they can be used for good or for ill. They can fall into the wrong hands. They can fall prey to our lack of self-knowledge and the acting out of our lower selves. Our shadow side can take something beautiful and make it ugly, can mask cruelty as righteousness.

I had liberated myself and was free to return to the late twentieth century, not to a time so much as to an emerging cosmic awareness—holistic and transpersonal. I no longer needed to contort myself into a pretzel as I tried to reconcile the unreconcilable.

We lived on different rungs on the ladder of the evolution of human consciousness, Irv and me. I continued on my path of spirit and left him to his.

A Czechoslovakian dissident, newly freed from the collapse of the Soviet system, was interviewed on Public Radio. When asked if his government should prosecute those who collaborated with the regime he answered, "I refuse to be a judge." His words became my motto of how to live going forward. I could not afford to be bitter and angry; I needed my energy for living.

What seemed at the time a rash and impulsive act, insisting on divorce right then and there rather than waiting until Raphie's adoption was final, turned out to be what saved us. Had I strategized and waited we would have been tied to Irv forever. Raphie would have grown up shuttling between two separate and incompatible worlds. He would have been controlled as harshly as I had been. Thankfully the wisdom of the greater knowing guided me to freedom.

I survived the patriarchy and came through.

During the following twenty-four years, we never heard a word from, nor saw, Irv again. There was never any interest evinced regarding Raphael, not even during Yom Kippur, the Day of Atonement, when one would have thought an apology for abandoning him would have been forthcoming.

Twenty-four years passed in silence; and then a strange event occurred. I had been writing this memoir for nearly two years, when, on a cold December night, I arrived at the story recounted here. I sat down at my computer and wrote:

"I made a hard bed for myself to lie on and then I had to lie on it."

The following morning early, my phone rang. It was my brother Sam calling, which was most unusual, since his custom was to phone me in the late afternoon on his way home from work. Registering his somber tone, I waited for his words with some trepidation.

"I regret to bring you this news," he said. "Irv Jackman passed away yesterday."

"Keep the company of those who seek the truth—run from those who have found it."
—VACLAV HAVEL

Diana and Raphie

CHAPTER 11

The Painting: Part 1

In the winter of 1945, as WWII wound down,
my father returned to Poland.

In the detritus of what was left of his family's former
large holdings, he found a small, one by three-quarter inch
photograph of his dearly beloved youngest sister, Franechka.

Making his way to the American Zone in Germany, where
the displaced persons gathered to seek immigration to the
West, he commissioned an artist to paint the
image found in the photo.

*H*AVING LEFT IRV AND THE patriarchy of black hatted men
behind, my first step was to find an affordable house and to make a
home for Raphie and me.

"It's a cold, cruel world out there," said Jane, the real estate agent, speaking to my situation, as she drove me to a small house in a neighborhood across the road yet several steps down the socio-economic ladder from the home we had lived in with Irv. Her words warned of a frightening reality I had not considered—that my little son and I would be of no consequence, on our own in an indifferent world.

Raphie, clad only in a diaper on that warm summer morning, awakened from his nap with a dazed look in his eyes. I held him to me, the heat of his body like a comforting hot water bottle pressed against my belly. We drove along in Jane's car, and saw, for the first time, the street, with its large leafy trees, where we would live. We stopped in front of a small bungalow, the sixth one from the corner. Raphie's weight in my arms anchoring me and providing ballast, we stepped into the living room of the house. Though small, the room was filled with light from a large wood-framed bay window, the light reflected in the hardwood floors.

Upstairs was an attic room converted into a bedroom, a dreamy space under the eaves, where I could pretend Jo March reclined on a settee, her fingers ink-stained, writing.

"I'll take it." I said.

But I was being banished—that is how it felt to me, shut out of the neighborhood I lived in with Irv, shunted into exile. With Irv, we lived in an established neighborhood of homes ranging from large and stately with expanses of green lawn to smaller ones standing side by side, all nestled together under a canopy of mature trees, with small parks scattered here and there. This enclave, a land mass of only one-and-one-half square miles, rested within the larger mega-metropolis of suburbs circling Detroit, each one housing its own religious, racial, ethnic, and socio-economic grouping. This particular neighborhood of university professors, of men and women in the professions, of NPR listeners, PBS watchers, and old lefty Democrats who drove modest cars and shopped at the local Farmer's Market, was a neighborhood where I felt at home.

Having finally attained it, a home in fitting surroundings, I was losing it in the divorce and found myself instead moving to a working-class neighborhood of small post-war bungalows, children smelling of urine running wild on the street, a mother's rough, gritty voice yelling out to her little son from her front porch, "Stop crying like a girl or I'll put a dress on you."

Pulling my baby safely to me, I closed the door behind us.

I was sliding down the ladder of what? upward mobility?—of manifesting the life I wanted, the life that lived within me. Looking down the ladder from the lower rungs to which I had fallen, I saw there was farther to fall. I needed to hang on for Raphie's sake.

The following year, in the desolate December of 1991, my father entered the season of his dying.

In the unremitting gray of that December, I traversed the snow-covered expanse of colorless white each day, putting one cold foot in front of the other for the sake of my little son, towards whom I felt overriding responsibility and love.

"Everything go work up nice, *Mamele*," was Daddy's message to me near the end. It did not seem so then, that everything would work out well, yet countless times in the years after he was gone, I reached for my father's words and sought to cleave to their meaning, as though his love for me was prophetic and could still save me from beyond the grave.

The painting is eleven inches wide by seventeen inches tall and bears an inscription in its lower right corner which reads: "Meyer, Gauting, 1948."

Meyer the artist, rendered the painting in Gauting,
a town near Munich, in the year 1948.

One evening, when I was at Sam's house, he walked in carrying the painting under his arm. When I saw it, my father's imminent demise and my demotion from adored daughter, favored child, registered in my belly.

"Mietek gave it to me," my brother said.

The painting was my father's only valued material possession. His act of ripping it away from their carefully arranged possessions in my parents' home and giving it to Sam was a powerful statement, its meaning transparent to me. Sam, not both of us, not me, was his true heir, the inheritor of his family legacy. I accepted Daddy's somber choice as a judgement, a decree from on high. I received it with a bowed head.

The previous February, Daddy had been unceremoniously sacked from his job in the warehouse of the supermarket chain previously owned by our American cousins. The chain of markets had recently been acquired by a large conglomerate which had no use for an eighty-nine-year-old part-time employee.

"It was like Hitler," Daddy said, of the way they informed him of his dismissal, and then escorted him down the long, dimly lit corridor and out of the building. For the first time since coming to America, he did not have the routine of work. Soon after, he began to complain of pain on the right side of his back, the pain, over time, becoming excruciating and robbing him of his patient, even-keeled nature.

Gray winter, the dark clouds hanging low in the sky, mirrored my internal climate. Only my little son's brightness, his face lit up from within, was able to penetrate the gray. I wanted to do right by him, to wrap him in love potent enough to make up for the father who walked away and the birth parents who faded into the ethers.

We were setting out for a nature hike in the woods on a Sunday morning. Raphie, two years old, soon coming upon three, hopped up into his car seat in the back of the car, game for this outing.

"Ets go, Mama." he said in his nasal, baby voice.

I was large and full with being Raphie's mother, finding I had a knack for mothering. Love for him exuded from my every pore, my embrace tender but not suffocating, an empathic attunement to my little son coming naturally to me. He lay on my belly on the couch in the living room as we listened to the call of the whales interlaced with the haunting response of Paul Winter's soprano sax. Or I read to him, book after book, never tiring.

In our nighttime ritual I sang his bedtime "songies"—

"Day is done, gone the sun, from the lakes, from the hills, from the sky. All is well, safely rest, God is nigh." *and*

"Row, row, row your boat, gently down the stream, merrily merrily merrily merrily, life is but a dream." *and*

"Evening has come, stars twinkle on high, guardian angels will watch over you, till morning is nigh..."

In Russian and in English I sang, "May there always be sunshine, may there always be heaven, may there always be mama, may there always be me."

The light of the bluebird of happiness, a blown-glass bird resting on a wooden stand with a light bulb underneath, glowed in the dark, and guardian angels sat on his dresser watching over him, so Raphie said.

We found the magical in the ordinary and surrounded ourselves with it.

But in my identity as a divorced woman, an only parent, I felt small and forlorn, afraid, and lonely. And this Sunday morning, I fled our house, taking Raphie with me, running from what felt like the starkness of just the two of us.

A walk in the woods, in the snow, maybe see a deer; that wintry Sunday my little son was ready for this next adventure. The woods beckoned as a place of stillness and beauty, a place of serenity and calm. As we drove to our destination, I envisioned Raphie run/walking ahead of me on the snowy path, delighting in wonders and discoveries, the pompom of his knitted blue hat bobbing along. The anticipation of such moments of pleasure was an impetus to set out away from the city, driving westward under an ominous, bleak sky.

Thick, wet, heavy snowflakes blanketed down, as the car entered the state park. I pressed forward into the snowstorm like a mule wearing blinders and pulling a heavy load, thinking we would wait out the snow with a hot cocoa in the park's rustic café—when we came to a rise in the road which the car could not manage, each attempted ascent sliding us backwards. The police were summoned and eventually pulled us out of the mess, pointing out that the tires on the car, a rather new Honda bought at a used car lot, were completely bald.

Later that day, when early evening had set in and streetlights and headlights were lighting the way, I turned the car away from the direction of home towards my parents' condo. Raphie and I were cold and tired, wrung out from the wait in the police car in the snow and from wandering in the mall for hours as new tires replaced the old ones, an anxiety-provoking expense. But I needed to avoid home for as long as possible, fearing home would smother me with feelings of fear and desolation. My parents' condo was the one place where I could arrive unannounced and know we would be welcomed, deriving comfort just by sitting and eating with them in the kitchen or watching television with my dad on the couch in the den.

Of late, however, I could not ignore that my parents had troubles of their own.

During a recent visit, I passed an excruciating few hours with them as the tension in the room crawled up my spine in prickly nervous tremors. My father, wearing his pajamas and a robe, sat in a blue armchair facing mine, a small round table between us. Mother walked in and out of the room carrying a tray with his tea and a light meal. I almost wrote that she "skittered" in and out of the room, skittered like a hapless domestic in a British country manor. Mrs. Gummidge came to mind, the "lone lorn creature" of Dickens' imagination, both she and my mom inveterate complainers, but I had never seen my mom obsequious before, not even for a moment.

I cannot remember the words spoken, cannot even approximate the way he expressed his dissatisfaction with her and her efforts to care for him, as though he was shooting darts at her feet, and she was jumping to avoid them. It is a snippet of memory without dialogue, and I would deem it impossible to have occurred at all, would doubt its veracity, so utterly different it was from anything that had transpired before—but for my very clear memory of nervous hysteria building within me.

I had always been thin-skinned—my father often saying in his heavy accent, pronouncing the "th" like the letter "d"—"You need a dicker skin, *Mamele,* a dicker skin." My boundaries were almost nonexistent, especially in regard to my mother. I was highly attuned to her, as though we lay on adjoining cots, transfusions of nervous impulses transmitting from her to me. That evening, I felt a frenzy of panic and rage building within her. I feared I would break out in hysterical laughter, not from mirth but rather from an intensity of watchfulness, expecting one or the other of them to erupt, causing the civil veneer of their marriage to shatter, and the undercurrents of the past forty years to spray across the room.

Meanwhile they asked me how things were going, and I jumped in and began talking. I talked and talked, "for fire and for *vasser*" as the Yiddish expression goes ("for fire and for water")—which I always took to mean talking as much and as fast as one can in order to save oneself, as though fire was chasing from behind and only if you kept the barrage of words coming would they make a barrier to protect you.

During the years of their marriage, my father had modeled a tolerant forbearance and wry humor towards my mother in the face of her challenging personality and unrelenting complaining and dissatisfaction. He found a way to cohabitate with her within a status quo of companionability more or less maintained, until now, when pain had taken over his body, and for the first time, he was short with her, critical, and even hostile.

While I knew she had it coming, and for years had been waiting for him to finally put her in her place, that evening my anxiety rose to new heights, and I braced myself for how far he would go. I was not sure which one of them I was rooting for as I sat in my chair, and she made feeble attempts to regain her ascendancy through the use of her old methods of put-downs and innuendos. He was, for the first time, indifferent, even impervious, and he did not let up on his push against her. I could scarcely register what was occurring, let alone process how overnight the old rules of conduct he had set for himself, and for my brother and I, were overturned. And though I cringed and had even felt revulsion at the old status quo, this new one, with the power structure overturned, was menacing as well.

When I was fifteen, and the old power structure was still firmly in place, I asked for my dad's protection. I told him how, since the revelations about my paternity, my mother would start in on my first father, talking about him and against him for hours. I asked Daddy to help me, to save me, to do something. Several days later, listening to them converse as I lay in bed, I heard how she outmaneuvered him, how he lost ground, until I nearly ran out into the kitchen to come to his aid, feeling guilty for putting him in this position. He could not protect me; he would not or did not know how to use her tactics, so it would be left to me to protect myself and even him.

We tried to protect one another, as it turned out, each of us behind the scenes speaking on behalf of the other. When the time came, he encouraged my decision to go to Israel. One afternoon, he actually said, without meeting my eyes—"You need distance from Mommy." When I lived in Israel, he would monitor the letters she wrote, insisting she tear up the ones where she was critical of me and my life. I know because she would write, "Daddy has gone to sleep now, and I am writing what I want to say without him seeing."

"She is a good mother," he would say, "a good, good mother. She loves you and Sammy and does everything for you." This was indisputably true. "But.." he would add:

"But she is like the cow who fills the bucket with her rich, fresh milk—only to kick the bucket over with her hind hoof, spilling all that she has given. That is Mommy, who loves you and Sammy so much and then spoils it with her words."

And Sammy, where was he in the family configuration? He often stood apart from the triangle of my mother, father, and I, hanging on but not part of it. Like Daddy said: "Everyone in our family was born under a different flag. I am from Poland, Mommy from Russia, you were born in Germany and Sammy is under the United States flag."

It was as though my brother came from a more wholesome, cleaner place. I wanted him to be untainted by the murky tragedies of Europe. I wanted to absorb the pain and leave him to be free, to be an American boy growing up in suburbia. All this was never spoken, but he seemed to know on his own to stay at his friends' houses, hang out with their parents and come home only for meals and bed. I needed to protect him and drew comfort knowing he was safely outside. Was the tariff I exacted for my sacrifice the right to be the favorite, the studious one, the one who cared about their suffering and was close to my parents? Not "rough and tough," like Sammy? I thought Sam was getting the better part of the bargain, but he may have felt otherwise.

The change in Daddy's behavior was stunning. He broke the rules without a by your leave, as though they had never been. Had he been harboring resentment towards her all these years? Had he been seething with anger from the beginning of their marriage when she betrayed him by kissing Yuzik in the back seat of the car? For in the past days, after all these years of silence, he revealed the incident to my brother, while I had known about it for years, the incident proudly recounted to me by my mother. And, dear God, please help me—was I just imagining a subtle undercurrent or was it so? Why did it feel as though I was somehow lumped in with her, included in his disillusionment, as though he was wishing he had never laid eyes on either one of us and had never taken us under his wing? Surely this was not so, the pain making him not himself, and I, feeling so deeply rejected and unwanted in any case, projected my fears onto him, feeling even my father does not love me.

Well, there had been the hurdle of my marriage to John, a Gentile, soon after I returned from Israel.

After the wedding ceremony my father and brother stood outside the Temple, both of them well turned out, impeccable in their suits and crisp shirts and ties, a look of distress on both their faces. That moment may have been my first glimpse of their father/son togetherness, an awareness of the alliance developing between them, my father sensing that my brother had adopted and inculcated his values and world view in a way that I had not. As John and I drove past on our way to the wedding reception, catching this glimpse of my father and brother pierced my heart—both for their sorrow and for their togetherness, in which, by marrying a non-Jew, I was no longer a part. Of course, or rather, as a matter of course, I did not give myself an accounting of what I was feeling, instead I allowed my glimpse of them to rush past and merge with the usual anxiety felt in my body and with the trees and other sights seen through the car window. I had a way of seeing without seeing, used for the first time on the day of the revelations of my paternity in the family living room when I was eleven years old. I survived that morning by blurring my vision, disconnecting what I saw with my eyes from what I felt in my heart, dismissing all of it. This *seeing without seeing* had become automatic, coming unbidden to shelter me from any threat I could not face.

There was no malice on my part in marrying John, no unkindness or slighting of my father's and brother's sensibilities intended. I was not oblivious to their pain. It was just that I assumed they would play their parts in the novel of my life that I was writing. My life unfolded at a remove from me. I stood back from it, as though behind a scrim, the scrim a defense keeping menacing realities at bay. But like every defense, it was destructive as it "protected," and nothing felt quite real to me.

Bringing John, a foreign element, into the family, caused a drastic altering of our intimate family circle. My father and brother were stymied, at a complete loss as to how to include this alien person. The mild coolness of John's demeanor, his modulated speech and patrician carriage, the blond hair and blue eyes, his high cheekbones and finely chiseled, proportioned body made John the quintessential Other.

We met in a psychology graduate program the year before, and after a brief acquaintance, I moved into the duplex he owned. We settled in together on the main level, while the upstairs flat was occupied by a single man who left his bike on the front porch. At the end of long days of work and school, we took walks along streets where John was comfortably at home. I felt disoriented, as though I had been parachute-dropped from Tel Aviv, where I had been living just months earlier, into this snow globe setting. The leaves, turning to fall colors, made rustling sounds as we walked, passing dignified homes decorated for Halloween—Christmas lights soon to follow.

My arm through John's, I imagined I could gain entry through my association with him, the surety of his belonging giving me a pass into this picture-perfect scene of idealized America. He, in turn, was enamored by his exotic Jewish girlfriend but soon sought to pare me down to a preppy look in the clothes he suggested I wear, hoping, I suppose, I would also rein in the animation of my voice and gestures. He won my heart—or at least what remained of my heart, as I had left a large portion of it behind in Tel Aviv—with the lunches he prepared for me to take to work, planting little fey cartoon drawings inside the brown bag, for me to find.

Of course, John was aware of my father and brother's distress. He had politely declined my father's suggestion that he convert to Judaism, his response growing a bit testy when my mother ignored his refusal and persisted in trying to talk him into it. He experienced their barely concealed rebuff as especially wounding, since he no longer had his own parents who had died in hideous and tragic circumstances.

John saved my family from the perplexity and angst of their dilemma by deciding, two months after our wedding, that he actually belonged with his ex-wife and her family who had held a place for him in their family circle since he was a teenager.

I thought my father's love for me was so steadfast that I could stretch and stretch its cord, even marry a Gentile, and it would not snap or sever. Now it was all catching up with me and I began to experience doubt. I married Irv, the uber-Jew at my father's urging, but then ended that disastrous union. My father was standing by me as steadfastly as before, yet I wondered what he must think of me, thrice married, and thrice divorced.

While Daddy had always been happy to see Raphie and me, always welcoming us with open arms, this Sunday evening, after the aborted walk in the woods in the snow, Daddy cut our visit short, saying his pain was getting the better of him and asked us to leave. Holding back tears, I picked up Raphie's toys from the floor and packed our bags. He must be dreadfully ill to ask us to go, I thought, yet the possibility lurked that he asked us to leave because he did not want us there. I knew this was untrue and that he loved us both, but I was no longer "positive sure," as he would say.

Wearing his blue pajamas and light blue cotton robe, my father walked with us to the top of the staircase leading to the front door, ushering us out of his house. I moved towards him as though under a hypnotic spell, the strange incident of the swollen lower leg suddenly coming to mind.

Several years earlier, my father's calf had swollen two to three times its normal size. Nothing the doctors suggested was helping. Within the various spiritual teachings and disciplines I studied, I had been exposed to a different way of thinking about the body and healing, concepts about a human energy field surrounding the corporeal body as we know it. Channeling currents of consciousness and love through the hands could bring about healing. I held this information lightly, but it occurred to me when I visited one afternoon that I might kneel down in front of my father, lay my hands on his grotesquely swollen calf, and give it a try.

The next day he phoned to tell me that the swelling was completely gone.

"What did you do? How did you do it?" he asked. "You are a witch."

Now, standing at the top of the staircase, I placed my hands on his back where the pain was localized, enfolding and camouflaging my actions within the goodbye hug we were sharing. He held me longer than usual, perhaps to make up for asking us to leave or he may have been hanging on for dear life, the pain draining him of the energy needed to let go and unlock our embrace. Meanwhile, pouring my love for him into my hands, streaming waves of energy and heat, I silently beseeched the angels for the cessation of his pain and for his healing.

Then we all kissed and hugged and Raphie and I departed.

The following morning, I phoned to ask how Daddy was feeling.

"No pain, *Mamele*, no pain at all," he said. 'It is as if someone touched me and the pain went away."

Several weeks later, after a hospitalization and a series of medical tests which proved inconclusive, a diagnosis of liver cancer was nevertheless assumed, and Daddy was sent home to die.

I had strongly disagreed with this plan to hospitalize but allowed my brother to override my wishes and opinions. Daddy's graceful aging, and the story of his survival during the war, made him seem invincible to my brother. He was coming upon his ninetieth birthday in two months' time and Sam wanted every effort to be made for Daddy to sail right past it and keep going. I, on the other hand, wanted to let nature take its course and keep Daddy comfortable at home. But I did not trust my knowing, deeming myself dark and negative, not optimistic like my brother, my life falling apart while his flourished, and thus, I surrendered my authority to him. My brother was the successful, prosperous one with a wife and baby son. He had produced an heir to my father's nearly extinct family, the bloodline ensured.

What weight did my opinion carry?

Daddy had always been a warrior on behalf of his health, monitoring his insulin intake religiously, never touching forbidden foods and remarkably never suffering the side effects one would expect from living with diabetes for forty years. His motto was: "I am my own best doctor," and he took this role very seriously. He exercised every day, was fit and trim and looked much younger than his years.

After the hospitalization he kept right on fighting—

"No pain, *Mamele*," he told me every day when I phoned or visited.

No pain, no need for pain medication, yet something was horribly wrong.

We sat in the den of my parents' condo, Daddy sitting on the sofa, and I on the floor facing him. He had me alone and caught me unawares. Earlier that morning, in a phone conversation with his doctor, he was told he no longer needed to concern himself with insulin injections.

Now he wanted to know.

"What is wrong with me, actually?" he asked.

I was extremely discomfited by this question, having been placed under strict orders by my mother and brother not to reveal his approaching demise to him. But it was diametrically opposed to my nature to lie or to keep things from my father. I looked up at him and did not speak, simply meeting his gaze. No words were exchanged but my silence answered everything he was asking.

"Mietek is finished." he said.

His sanguine attitude towards death had been a source of comfort and reassurance to me over the years. "No one lives forever; we are born to die, *Mamele,*" he would say.

So I was surprised when I phoned their home the next morning and my mother told me in an accusatory tone that my father had a very rough night. He was shouting and angry, and when she asked him what was wrong he said, "Ask Diana." Insinuation, innuendo— in her cold disapproval, I received the message—Daddy is terrified, afraid to die, and I am to blame.

Franechka's gentle gaze looking down upon us from the wall above the couch in the living room of our family home was a permanent and poignant fixture of my childhood.

The vivid colors in the oil painting depict a bucolic scene.

A young woman is perched demurely on what seems to be a large sawed-off tree trunk or boulder, a jacket casually draped over it, a flower-strewn pasture in the background.

Franechka is wearing a white dress, a gold wristwatch, and a kerchief on her head; the kerchief painted a vivid red, drawing the eye to it.

Peering into the original photograph with a magnifying glass, one sees Franechka's broad forehead and her pretty, delicate, face with its full-lipped mouth.

Daddy's strength was ebbing and draining away, this fighter for survival now bowed in the face of defeat. The end was approaching, and today, for the first time, he could not leave his bed. A subdued light entered the room from the window as he lay, the pastel sheets freshly laundered, the light blue comforter gently covering him. Sam and I sat next to Daddy's bed, our bodies half in shadow. Daddy's soft face with its benevolent expression had collapsed in upon itself since yesterday, the skin cleaving tighter to the bones, giving it an angular cast. His nose, which had been fleshy wore a pinched, thin look, his blue eyes and mild gaze was now piercing and dark.

Turning to my brother, he said:

"Sammy, I know where you come from. You are Shlomo, ben (the son of) Moshe, ben Shlomo."

Then he turned to me and said, "But I don't know where you come from."

"Daddy," my voice strangling out of the narrow passageway that was left of my throat, pleading: "Daddy, you know me, you know where I come from."

"No! Sammy is Shlomo, ben Moshe, ben Shlomo, but I don't know where you come from."

Within seconds, his words spread, seeping like black ink over porous cloth, leaving a dark indelible stain. The tattoo of words, "I don't know where you come from," sank in, more than skin-deep, sank into my muscles and bones, leaving an imprint down to my core.

He made his pronouncement like Jehovah, the Biblical smiting God, a wrathful deity, as though he were on high, standing on the bed, pointing his finger—the All-Seeing One—letting me know, while he still had time and breath, judging and proclaiming, that I am a stranger to him after all, not his.

The cold, bitter wind of December blew over me as I stepped outside onto the balcony. There would never be enough wind and fresh air to wipe clean the words I had just heard. I could barely stand in this nadir moment of my life.

Sam joined me out on the balcony. I avoided his eyes, feeling separated behind a filmy cowl; an outcast. I was ashamed and repugnant, a filthy, abandoned baby left on the convent steps, uttering disembodied words about being rejected, sending my agony across the divide:

"Every man I love and am close with betrays and rejects me."

"Why did you say that?" Sam asked angrily of our dying father. "How could you say that?"

Daddy tried to pull himself up to a sitting position but could not.

"I didn't mean it." Daddy said. "I didn't mean anything. I love you, *Mamele*, I love you."

"It's ok, Daddy. You have one adopted child and one biological child. I only have an adopted child, so I can't know how you feel…" I babbled, trying to reassure him, to fix his agitation, to take away his distress.

I could not make his words go away. I was left to decipher their meaning; the felt meaning being that on his deathbed, my father was abdicating his relationship with me. He was like my mother now, kicking over the pail of milk, only much worse, this being a deathbed scene and no more milk could ever be offered again. Who is the mistaken cow after all, Daddy? It was too late to ask him what meaning his words held for him, how he arrived at such musings and why he felt the need to utter them.

My sense of belonging to the world had been eroding and was now slipping away. Really, when I thought about it, I was not fully biologically related to anyone, as the titles, "daughter, mother, sister, niece" would suggest, not to anyone on this earth except my mother, a relation I feared resembling. My father was not biologically related to me, neither was my son. My brother was my half-brother, my nephew a quarter. Fenia, who I thought of as my aunt, introduced me as her cousin. I was flying untethered off the earth, only my love for my son reminding me I had a role to play and a reason to stay.

The next morning, Daddy was unconscious and unresponsive. That evening, we sat on his bed, Sam's arm around Daddy's shoulder, mine holding his legs. This was the peaceful, beautiful death I wanted for him, to match the story he told me of his first memory of life:

"I was a little boy wearing a blue velvet suit. I walked into the room and everyone hugged me and kissed me."

He was leaving the earth with this same love surrounding him, dying in his own home, in his own bed, his children at his side, pain free. Yet I let the sanctity of the moment slip away. The lights were on, not dimmed; Sam's wife Laurie and a cousin were also hanging out on the bed, and we were conversing. I cannot account for this— why we began reminiscing as if Daddy wasn't there, as if he couldn't hear, although hearing, I have learned, is the last of the senses to go.

It should have been just Sam and me, the lights in the room dimmed, no conversation—rather sitting quietly with Daddy, ushering him on to the next steps in his journey. How did the bedside vigil become a conversation rather than a sacred accompaniment ushering Daddy out of this world? I only know I retreated behind my defense, seeing without seeing. As the passing moments became more and more unreal, a visual screen smeared with Vaseline separated me from myself, from Daddy, from Daddy dying. Pulling back behind the screen was the only way I could bear this moment. Powerful fear, powerful pain, powerful love—I could not hold it all, so I withdrew deep inside myself, too far away to take hold and to take charge, the moments and Daddy slipping away, unable to create what I wanted for him and what I knew should be.

Daddy grew agitated, his breathing grew more labored and then one last whoosh of out breath, no more in breath and he was gone.

I grieved like most of us do for the loss of a beloved parent. The animal grief of my body registered pain and loss. But I found I was unable to wrap myself in the comfort of the old love and happy memories. Instead all the good was overshadowed, almost erased, by the memory of the winter sun spilling its weak light into a room immersed in shadow and by my father letting me know he does not know where I come from. It was as though the loving relationship we shared, and the profound heartfulness I had always felt from and towards him, was hidden inside a cave. A huge boulder had been moved in front of the mouth of the cave blocking its entrance, even camouflaging the memory of its existence. I took his last words as gospel and negated all the rest. I had not thought the father who lived within me capable of hurtful words of disavowal. Was I using his words and the meaning I attributed to them to shield myself from the pain of his loss?

I continued to appreciate the loving father he had been. He had come into my life at a crucial moment, rescued and saved me, and was very kind and good to me throughout, earning my lifelong gratitude. Yet what was affected in the end, was not only how I felt him within myself, but how I felt about myself. At the end of his life, I lost the certainty of being beloved by him, lost our sweet, sweet connection, lost the conviction of my place in his heart and in his life. It felt as though a pillar of my identity crumbled.

Photo of Franechka

CHAPTER 12

The Painting: Part 2

For nine years, the painting lay on its side behind the
television in my brother and sister-in-law's bedroom.

RAPHIE'S FACE IS FLUSHED, HIS body hot, and the sickly,
sour smell of strep throat is on his breath. Bending over his crib,
my chest and belly tense tighter, ramping up the anxiety I felt when
I woke up. He needs attention and care while I have nine clients
on my schedule. Canceling and rescheduling is a logistical hurdle,
besides, we need the money. *Don't let him see your panic*, I think,
*don't let him feel it. He needs something to drink, a compress to cool
him, his medicine. I can't, I just can't. You have to. Move!*

Mom stands in the landing next to my kitchen with her coat
on. She will take care of Raphie, and I will go to work.

"Why aren't you coming in? What's wrong?" I ask.

"I can't get close to Raphie."

"What are you saying?"

"Strep infection is poison for my heart," she says.

"You drove all the way to my house to tell me you are not coming in? Why didn't you just say you couldn't help me when I phoned?" I need to be at work in an hour. "OK, just go, leave, I will figure it out."

Guilt drove her to my house, yet she knew she would not stay. The politics and diplomacy of this moment are beyond me. I have nothing available with which to dive into the undercurrents sloshing and roiling between us.

I gather Raphie's medicine, his blanket and pillow. I grab his "micky," a blue thermal blanket. Jessica, his stuffed raccoon, will come with us as well. I fill the pink cooler with food and put his juice and picture books in a bag. I dress us both and carry Raphie to the car, buckle him into his car seat, make several trips back and forth to the house, strap on my seat belt and drive off.

With Raphie in my arms, I cross the parking lot and walk up the stairs to the second floor where our suite of offices is located. I lay him down on a couch in an unused office adjacent to mine. I return to the car, making several trips, moving as quickly as I can. I put his pillow under his head and cover him with his blanket, place his "micky" on top, put the juice, the antibiotic, and the food in the refrigerator, put Jessica in his arms and his picture books within reach.

My first client waits in the waiting room and my workday begins. During breaks between clients, I check in on Raphie. He lies quietly in the small windowless office sheltering him; not demanding and not complaining. Mothering elicits primal feelings in me, primarily the need to protect. Images of pre-history arise; we have found shelter from the elements in this dry cave. Momentarily safe, I wrap my child in furs and hold him close. This fantasy is profoundly satisfying somehow, a feeling of refuge that reaches down into my bones, calming me.

My workday ends at ten p.m. I bundle Raphie into his jacket and hat, balance him on one arm and his pillow, blanket, and micky in the other, as we descend into the cold, dark, wintry night. Leaving Raphie wrapped in the blanket, buckled into his car seat, I lock the car doors, and run back upstairs to collect the cooler, the bottle of apple juice, his medicine, his picture books, and Jessica, the raccoon; then, fast as I can, I run back.

I cannot believe I am standing out here in this deserted parking lot, alone with a sick child. Resentment rises in me towards the others, the women in my life who are not standing here in this cold parking lot in the dark. They are safely nestled at the family hearth, children asleep in their beds, protective husbands by their sides. Alongside the resentment, I notice a perverse pride, a feeling of superiority. There is pleasure in this pain, the pleasure of prevailing, the pleasure of the mama bear keeping her cub safe, the pleasure of the strength I draw from within myself. None of those coddled women would have managed, I think, or maybe they would have. But they do not need to, they do not need to prove their mettle as I do.

Life has finally caught up with me. There are no more short cuts allowing me to avoid the tough challenges, challenges like providing for a child, shoveling snow, raking leaves, grocery shopping, and cooking.

I pick Raphie up from day care, walk into the market with him, lift him into the shopping cart, fill the cart with groceries, come out of the store to find the windshield frozen, scrape the windshield while snow falls into the collar of my coat, lift the grocery bags into the trunk, carry them into the house, put the groceries away, and cook dinner. I clean the kitchen and then give Raphie a bath. Finally, I sing his bedtime songs to him.

It was not that I was lazy before nor was I a prima donna, although others may have deemed me so. It was that my energy and attention were occupied elsewhere, as it had been since age thirteen. The fear messages of dis-ease in my body augmented the voices in my head, voices that negated everything about me; an incessant, enervating diatribe.

Whatever I was able to do or accomplish was in spite of the cacophony of voices and the feelings of dread in my body. I learned to allocate my physical and mental strength for whatever was most necessary and to leave the rest. Even after an eight-hour night's sleep, I felt drowsy the next day, and anxiously scanned my schedule for a chance to nap, to escape from the storm in my head.

Now I was up against the wall of my life, and I had to face it. I flirted with suicide, but even in this, I knew I was trapped. Raphie was here and I would not abandon him to strangers. Seductive thoughts crept in though, such as, if I were gone he would be adopted by a two-parent family and have a better life than I could give him. I made the decision over and over again. There was no suicide, no leaving. Life had me in its grip—tough and seeming beyond my capabilities.

In the midst of this, help came from unexpected sources, showed up in otherworldly ways and provided inspiration to keep going.

During the first spring living in our house, rain poured ceaselessly for four days, the yard growth like a rainforest threatening to overtake us. I paid the babysitter extra money to mow the lawn and averted my eyes from the rest.

Until one day, in the latter part of that first summer, something caught my attention. Two large planters with scrawny weeds growing in them were left on the front deck by the previous owner. One morning, three purple petunias showed up among the weeds. No friend or family member had come by to cheer me up with purple petunias, yet there they were. The flowers glittering in the sun, their purple petals laced with gold, were emissaries of light. Each time I walked past the living room window and looked out, I felt them beckoning. We need water, we need space for our roots to grow. Come outside and tend to us.

I ventured into the garage looking for my father's gardening tools which had somehow been bequeathed to me. I pulled a narrow trowel out of the pile and used it to turn the dirt in the planters, releasing a loamy smell. The tenderness and solicitude I felt towards the flowers were akin to caring for Raphie—mother love, a rich new facet of me. I looked up from my work, gazing around at the house and yard, at Raphie playing in the dirt with his plastic gardening tools. The memory of the cave, its protective nature, had expanded to include our yard, this little hacienda; my domain providing me an opportunity to tend and foster, to belong to the earth and the seasons.

My neighbor helped pull out old bushes. We both caught vicious cases of poison ivy, but I kept on going and planted new bushes.

"You are planting too close to the end of the season," my father had said. "The bushes will not survive."

He would be dead in a matter of months, but the next spring, pink flowers bloomed in the bushes.

I saw a woman on the American frontier. She was shading her eyes, surveying her large holding, her ranch. She appeared to me during a past life recall session at a Holotropic Breathwork workshop. I sensed her worry—her husband had gone over the mountain pass to purchase supplies and should have returned by now. I saw that he was caught in a freak snowstorm and did not make it out. The woman was left alone on the homestead and was determined to hold on to it. In the next scene, she is an old woman looking out at the land. Rooted to this landscape, she embodies the majesty of her accomplishment. She is a woman of substance, honed by tragedy and grit.

I rent a Rototiller—who had even heard that word before? I fertilize the soil. Putting in long workdays, I plant a perennial garden at the front of the house and tend to all the flower beds and plantings in the front, side, and back yards. Sweat pours off me; I am dirty and tired and my body aches. At moments, I feel sorry for myself. I feel afraid and overwhelmed and then I call forth the woman on the western frontier. Fortified by the "memory" of her, I press on. Lifting bags of mulch from the trunk of the car and carrying them across the yard, I pull from her strength and resolve.

I look up at the sky and think—Daddy must be rolling over in his grave seeing me, his *Mamele*, working like a "*fornal*," a word he used (was it Polish or Yiddish?) to describe a common laborer, a somewhat debased person. He did everything he could to protect me from a moment like this. But now? He is proud of me, I think.

I amaze myself.

I may be less "feminine" than I was before, but a me is being established, a person I can count on. It is a painstaking hacking and carving into a marble slab, seeking the outlines of a new person— and at the same time, the darkness of depression threatens to sink the entire enterprise.

Depression was turning into the dominant narrative of my life. I came to think of it as an autoimmune disease, the self attacking the self, a brutal turning against oneself from the inside, a relentless, implacable, internal enemy. I was not safe for a moment. Every stimulus—hearing a friend's plans for weekend enjoyment, a couple walking in front of me at the mall, women laughing in a coffee shop, a visit with family—could become the trigger for a vicious attack. They did life right, I did it wrong. They are good, I am bad. What I can never have, who I can never be, failings and shortcomings, self-hate, self-blame, shame, blame of others, perseverating about a perceived slight or lack, ricocheting resentment directed one way or another. From the moment I woke in the morning, I was bombarded.

On rare occasions, usually when taking a walk, I could step outside my mind for a moment and observe it. The only way to survive would be to stop thinking. I walked along and each time a thought arose, I shook my head back and forth—"no thought, no thought, no thought." This worked for several blocks, when a new, more "compelling" thought entered and within seconds I was off, far down the tracks of the entrained mind, my point of embarkation a speck in the distance, far behind.

Word of a new drug, a drug called Prozac, was touted as a revolutionary approach to fixing the symptoms of depression. People who had suffered from depression for years were experiencing seemingly miraculous breakthroughs. Science had tamed the monster.

For the first time, I thought there might be a way out. Prozac could put me on a level playing field with everyone else. The depression is not my fault, I learned, not something I need to work with and work on and figure out, not neurosis. It is my brain chemistry which needs adjusting, the neurotransmitters must be set right.

I asked the psychiatrist on staff at our clinic to write a prescription for me. I expectantly downed the pill each morning, waited out the initial six-week adjustment period for the drug to kick in. Month followed month. The depression darkened and worsened; anxiety rose to new heights. My system was not responding to Prozac. I was not one of the lucky ones.

With time, I found a reputable psychopharmacologist, a Dr. T. who was kind, respectful, modest, and unassuming. He heard my story, took one look at Raphie, and decided never to charge me for his services. We began with Klonopin which, unfortunately, bonded with my brain cells in such a way that I was reduced to managing my anxiety by walking up and down the sidewalk as fast as I could, repeating my name, age, and address out loud in order to orient myself and hold on.

Over the course of the next few years, I tried every depression treating drug available—the other SSRI's in the Prozac family, Wellbutrin, and the old Tricyclics with side effects like weight gain, dry mouth, and constipation. On and on it went, trying a drug, giving it some time, starting low with the aim of reaching a clinical dose, not feeling well enough to bump up higher, too risky to jeopardize my shaky daily functioning with slamming in a full dose from the get-go. Weening off the failed trial, trying another medication, hope rising that this one will work. Constant phone calls back and forth to Dr. T.—he knew my phone number by heart and I, of course, knew his. He became my lifeline, and although he was unfailingly kind to me, I felt tethered and dependent. He knew what was happening inside of me and what it meant better than I did. I held on to him for dear life, clutching the tow rope he extended, but this dependency on him enfeebled and undermined me.

One snowy Saturday morning in February, Raphie and I set out for Orchestra Hall.

We had not originally been invited to join the Detroit Youth Symphony Concerts subscription bloc with our friends and their children. This was another challenge of those years—the fear of being left out and left behind. It often seemed that my pain was too much for people. Depression was a repellent, whereas, I thought, if I had cancer, people would go out of their way to be kind and helpful. Stop being so self-involved, self-pitying, and spoiled. These were judgements thrown at me, reinforcing my belief that I am bad and wrong.

I observed and tried to imitate the behavior of my friends. I longed to live in my body as they lived in theirs. I did not understand that this was impossible. I did not understand the effects of trauma on the body.

One example stands out in particular. My friend Deborah and I were taking a walk with the children. Two of the girls and Raphie walked alongside, and the baby was wheeled in her stroller. My attention was fixed on the childrens' small feet inside their small shoes as they walked near the stroller's wheels. My body was braced, alert with tension, preparing for the jolt, the moment when one of the children would collide with the stroller and fall. Deborah chatted, the sun warmed us, the children were beautiful beings of light and flesh, but my eyes were looking down. And then Augusta's foot hit the stroller wheel. I flinched and jumped. Augusta stumbled and righted herself. The occurrence did not even register on Deborah's radar as we continued walking.

I asked my friends if we could please be included in the subscription and now we were on our way to one of the monthly Saturday concerts, traveling on the far-right lane of three lanes on the I-75 freeway, heading south. Near Eight Mile Road our car rounded a curve and hit a patch of black ice. It rolled into a spin, swayed left, then right and then turned around completely. The car, still moving at speed, was now lunging towards oncoming traffic. The steering wheel was loose and unresponsive in my hands. An olive-green colored jeep coming towards us was the last thing I saw before I let go of the steering wheel, shut my eyes, and braced for the impact.

The next sensation was of the car gently lifting and then being tenderly set down, as though placed on a bed of cotton, on the shoulder of the road, still facing oncoming traffic. The only sound I heard was the rush of blood in my ears.

Two men appeared at my driver side window. They were both out of breath, one wore a large gold cross, the other radiated warmth and benevolence.

"How did you do that? How did you do it?" they asked.

"What? How did I do what? I didn't do anything."

"We didn't know what we'd find when we came to the car," one of them said, looking through the window into the back seat.

"Is the little one alright?"

I turned around to look at Raphie. He was sitting in his car seat, not speaking, not crying.

The two men continued to stare at me in astonishment, as if I were an apparition, one with magical powers.

Declining their offers to call for help, I asked for their assistance in turning the car around back into traffic, so I could proceed to my destination.

I sought to steady my shaking legs, as holding hands, Raphie and I made our way down the long aisle of the auditorium in Orchestra Hall, to our seats. When our friends Deborah and David and their little girls arrived some moments later, I told David—"We nearly had an accident. We were saved by an angel."

"We saw your car," David said. "You were turned around facing traffic on the shoulder of the road. We exited the freeway to come to your aid, but when we returned to the spot where you had been, your car was gone. So we came on to Orchestra Hall."

The music began in the darkened auditorium, but I was deaf to the sound, my thoughts and attention circling elsewhere, back to the moments in the car, the loss of control, the spinning, the jeep bearing down at speed.

As the moments passed, the warmth in the easeful dark of the auditorium soothed me, the music made its way to my ears, and I found my awareness rising through the roof of the concert hall into an imaginary starry night sky. From this vantage point, the moments in the car—the floating sensation and the soft landing—began to seem not a punishment but rather a promise, comfort letting us know we are not alone. Our deliverance began to seem as though something, somewhere, was trying to make itself known to us.

After the concert, we drove home. As we pulled into the driveway of our house, a momentary parting of the clouds allowed the sun's rays to shine on an object laying on the stoop by the door. I bent down to pick it up and set it on the kitchen counter as we rushed off to the activities of the rest of our busy day. That evening, something on the kitchen counter caught my eye. It was the object which had glistened on the step in the brief moment when the sun broke through. I picked it up and saw I was holding a gold cross.

I asked everyone who frequented my home—the woman who cleaned, the postman, the babysitters, friends, clients—whether someone had misplaced or lost a gold cross. When no one claimed it, I placed it in a small silver box on a table next to my chair in my home office. On rare occasions, when I shared the story of the averted accident, I reached over and opened the silver box, showing the listener the cross resting there.

I lay in bed at night and allowed my thoughts to return to the unfolding events of that day. I wondered why, if it were so, Jesus would have saved two Jews, Raphie and me. Or was it an angel who saved us? Perhaps it was a cosmic glitch, a hiccup between the cosmos and the material world, an accident not meant to happen, one needing to be speedily aborted. During nights of sleeplessness, I would lean heavily into the memory of those moments, feel the car spinning out of control, remember the sensation of being gently

lifted onto the shoulder of the freeway and see the two men standing next to the window.

The memory sustained and reassured me. I could not make ra-
tional sense of what happened, nor could I dismiss it, and in this
way, the spiritual realm opened itself to me. I told Raphie we were
saved for a reason. But I wondered if the occurrence itself was the
reason—the opening of perception into the All That Is, manifesting
as rescue and comfort when it was most needed.

In August of 2001, Yoni, a friend from Israel, came to visit. One
evening after dinner, he and I sat across from one another at the
kitchen table. Gesturing, drawing diagrams, I described the curve
in the road, the expressway lanes, the shoulder on the side, and the
car rolling into a spin. I brought Yoni down into the canyon of the
freeway and told him the story of Raphie's and my deliverance. As
dusk deepened, I finished speaking and Yoni and I sat in silence.
Then I walked into my office to collect the small silver box. When I
brought it into the kitchen and opened it, the cross was gone.

One more "coincidence" became a touch stone for me, another
sign from the other side. The Dalai Lama was coming to Ann Arbor
to speak. I bought a ticket, weeks in advance, and pinned it on my
corkboard. Raphie would stay overnight at a cousin's house, and I
would drive to Ann Arbor with friends, make an outing of it, have
dinner together after the Dalai Lama's presentation.

When I left the house, I took my ticket off the corkboard, put
it in my purse, and drove to Michael and Iris's house, where the
friends had decided to meet. Brian, who lived in Ann Arbor, would
join us at Hill Auditorium. Waiting to leave, June and I sat sunning
ourselves on the stoop of Michael's house. She asked what my seat
number was. I opened my wallet to look at my ticket, but it was

gone. I rushed home and also to the bank where I had stopped to withdraw cash, but the ticket was nowhere to be found.

My friends urged me to come along with them in any case. Raphie was already settled for the evening, so why not take advantage of my freedom? I could sit in Border's Book Shop while they listened to the Dalai Lama and then we could have dinner together afterwards. Wrapped in a dark funk of self-pity in the back seat of the car, I brooded and oozed resentment towards them for their impervious wellbeing.

When we arrived at the steps of Hill Auditorium, I decided to stand in line with the others and throw myself on the mercy of Jewel Heart, the organizers of the Dalai Lama event. I had bought a ticket after all. I hoped they would believe me. A woman behind us heard me telling my friends the plan.

"I have an extra ticket," she said. "Here, you can have it."

We entered the lobby and ushers showed us to our seats. June was led away first, then Brian, but Iris, Michael and I were directed to ascend and ascend, one flight after another. Finally, at the top of the auditorium we were led to our seats—and astonishingly, my seat was right next to Michael's, elbow to elbow. Iris sat to his left, then Michael, then me, and to my right my ticket benefactor. She and her husband were truck drivers from Florida. He had been called in to work at the last minute, so she came to Ann Arbor without him. We were sitting up high, and the Dalai Lama was seated far below. In my effort to assimilate all that had happened, his words barely registered. Until he said: "My religion is kindness, kindness is my religion." And ever since that day kindness has been my religion as well.

One evening during a break between clients, I phoned my mother who was babysitting for Raphie.

"He needs to see you," she said, "I am bringing him to your office."

I don't remember why I agreed to this when I knew I had three more clients to see. Sensing that she wanted to spend the rest of the evening with her new man friend, I might have felt I had no choice. Or perhaps I was listening to a more prescient voice within me.

I remember the feel of Raphie's small hand in mine, how small he seemed and how tall I felt in comparison, as we walked together from the waiting room along the hall corridors with their muted light, towards my office. I sensed profound relief in Raphie, in his little body when he saw me— a coming home to a safe harbor.

My office was lit by a table lamp. I sat down on my chair, a blue upholstered recliner, and lifted him onto my lap. He lay crosswise, the heft of him, with his head against my breast, my hands supporting his body, as he rested quietly before falling asleep.

You are the greatest gift life has given me, I thought, as I smoothed his hair, each caress a prayer and a benediction. *I would do anything to care for and protect you. You are a precious being. My heart is overflowing with love for you. Every second of these moments and hours is a blessing.*

Holding a child in my arms was of course, a highly unorthodox and even risky way to receive clients. Reason says I should have either cancelled my evening schedule or insisted my mother keep Raphie at home. Yet this experience unfolded as in a dream—the lamp-lit evening, the quiet in the clinic, the solidity of Raphie's body in my arms. As I held him, I felt deeply nourished, as though I had been starving and was only now partaking of sustenance.

The love state we inhabited seemed to have a salutary effect on all who entered my office that night. One client in particular, a young man in his thirties who still lived at home with his parents, had never had a relationship with a woman. During the session, he connected the tableau of mother and child sitting before him with an awareness. He was certain, he said, he could feel it in his body, that he had never been held in this way. He cried, as he spoke of the coldness of his mother and the coldness within himself. He related this coldness to the absence of intimate relationship in his life.

I've thought of that evening in my office many times over the years, but now it is releasing a new meaning, a different import. Raphie was the gift from the heavens that showed me my infinite capacity to love. And whatever else happened or was lacking, whatever shortcomings I had or have as a mother or as a person—I had provided during many such moments, a dip into the sea of profound unconditional body-embracing, full-hearted Love. Why hadn't I owned this before? In my constant effort to improve and fix myself, I hadn't seen what was right before my eyes. That I was capable of profound, tender, selfless, unconditional love which brought healing to the other and to myself. This love was not me or mine, rather it was and is universal love, a bridge between our human and our divine selves.

One night when Raphie was three years old, a "squirrel's nest" appeared at the foot of my bed.

"I need to sleep in a squirrel's nest," he said.

Taking a red futon cushion out of my closet, bringing sheets and blankets, a comforter, and his "micky" from downstairs, Raphie assembled his nest. When he had it just the way he wanted it, he snuggled in and went to sleep.

Nights of repose, of profound tranquility, settled upon me. A web of contentment spun to envelop us both, a warm cocoon of refuge. This was the nature of our being together—a healing sanctuary.

And when the time was right, some months later, Raphie listened to his inner knowing and returned to his bedroom downstairs to sleep in his own bed.

Raphie's presence in my life opened the world to me anew. We spread out a map on his bedroom floor, a map showing the planet's animals and the continents where they lived. Every month, a Zoobook arrived in the mail, and we pored over it. We studied the lives and habits of the animal kingdom. In this way, we traversed the globe together.

Up north, on the shores of Lake Michigan, Jessica, the raccoon "told" us about the migration of her tribe to their summer hunting grounds, right here where we were standing, on the shore of the Great Lake. Creativity unknown to me, dormant within, sprung forth; Raphie's and my synergy calling forth stories and tales serving to spark our imaginations and entertain us.

The summer following Raphie's second grade year, we traveled to Paris to visit Uri. For months before the trip, we had been reading about the lives of the artists and had been looking at pictures of their paintings. At the *Musée D'Orsay*, the *Orangerie*, the *Louvre*, Raphie moved from room to room, recognizing "old friends," exclaiming at the paintings and sculptures he had seen in his books, now come to life. We played handball and read *The Sign of the Beaver* aloud to one another. And Raphie painted, painted, and painted.

From the time he was three years old, Raphie painted and drew. He wrote and illustrated an alphabet book of sea life and also a picture book about a newt who had *"no, no, No friends"* who then met a salamander that cried and a heron that became his friend. He fashioned a tableau out of colored clay dough—a sculpted scene of a tree, a pond, a duck and squirrels, a platform "teeming with life," he said.

I had been as dry as the desert before Raphie brought art into my life. Now I could only marvel and supply him with all the art supplies he requested. He wore his soccer uniform to art class after school and then hastily put on his shin guards and cleats in the car, as we raced to soccer practice. Indoor and outdoor soccer, basketball, books, painting, and drawing, all lived harmoniously within him.

After my father's death, the painting of his sister Franechka, with its eye-catching bright red kerchief, lay on its side behind the television stand in my brother and sister-in-law's bedroom. Sighting a rare glimpse of it, I sorrowed for its neglected status, its downfall from its previous hallowed place in my parents' home—but I felt powerless to save it. The painting went the way of other painful losses in my life, into the dark place of ache in my chest. In the years since my father's death, the hurt of having been bypassed for stewardship of the painting and my father's dismissive words to me when he was on his deathbed, had burrowed deeply into the fabric of my being.

I wanted to ask my brother to share the painting with me, but I didn't dare, fearing a "no" response from him would lead to a rupture, an irreparable breach in my feelings towards him, and thus in our relationship. So I allowed the hurts to fester and the painting to languish in its forlorn place behind the television.

Until one evening, nine years after my father's death, when our family returned to my brother's house after attending the Ne'ilah service which ends Yom Kippur.

"Sam?" I asked. "You know the painting of Franechka you have upstairs. Would you consider sharing the painting with me—say, six months here, six months at my house?"

"Daddy gave it to me," he replied.

What angel of mercy gave me the temerity to take it a step further?

"I know, but I need to share it, to have it at my house for part of the time. I need it for my healing."

Surprisingly, I heard "Ok," as he walked out of the room.

Moments later he returned with the painting, which he had placed inside a white plastic garbage bag.

"You can have it. It means more to you than it does to me."

That night, I hung the painting in my bedroom, on the wall facing my bed. As I gazed at it, ripples of joy moved up and down the length of my body. By retrieving the painting, I had taken a tentative step towards rapprochement with my father—calling back into myself the love and devotion we had shared with one another. The breach between us was no longer a total eclipse obliterating everything that had gone before.

When I was ready to separate from the painting for a short while, I took it to an art restorer. He made necessary repairs and cleaned the painting. I wanted to buy a new frame, but as we tried different pairings, it became clear the one my father had originally chosen was actually the one most fitting. By opting for the same frame my father had selected, I felt as though I was retracing his footsteps. The measure of peace and redemption the painting brought him became mine as well.

I restored the painting of Franechka to a place of prominence, front and center, on my mantelpiece. It felt as though Franechka, the one in the painting but also her soul, was blessing me—honoring me for rescuing her and claiming myself.

The Painting

PART FOUR

Breaking the Spell

CHAPTER 13

Healing Steps

A SUNDAY, EARLY AFTERNOON.

THE DAY BURDENED BY A cover of dull, overhanging clouds. Riding my bike through the encompassing gray, I cried and rode, rode and cried. I had recently gathered the painting of Franechka into my embrace, an act filled with love and hope. Her presence in my home, on the fireplace mantle, was a step forward, a psychological breakthrough. Yet, as often happened with breakthroughs and steps forward—Franechka and I taking one another into our hearts could not counteract the relentless self-critical thoughts and anxious gut churnings circulating through my body and mind.

I pedaled past outdoor restaurants filled with laughing people enjoying their Sunday brunch, past couples holding hands, heads tilted towards each other. Witnessing their pleasure, sharp knives of regret pierced my heart; this felt like proof of all that is wrong with me and right with everyone else. The unattainable normal accentuated my own private hell. Everything hurt.

Five years into one failed anti-depressant drug trial after another left me trembling, crying, and enfeebled.

A comforting possibility arose as I pedaled across Eleven Mile Road. Tonight, after Raphie falls asleep, I will go to the garage, close the door, start the car, and climb into the back seat. A pillow under my head, my green comforter tucked around me, I will be safe in my cozy nest. An alluring reverie as I rode—the exhaust fumes would lull me into a final, restful sleep.

But what then? The conclusion was unconscionable. For what of the next morning? Raphie—standing alone on our driveway, Raphie panic-stricken, terrified . . .

STOP.

It's either him or me. It has to be him. It has to be Raphie that matters.

I watched myself in wonder that evening as I was able to go about my routine, cook dinner, and sit at the kitchen table, eating and talking with Raphie. I watched as I completed the tasks of Sunday night, as I prepared for the coming school and work week.

Finally, I made my way upstairs to my bedroom.

In bed that night, I excavated down to where my animal nature dwelt, to raw survival. Survival, and then not merely survival. I dug deeper—to inspiration and guidance.

After five years of failed trials with anti-depressants, it was time to free myself from my dependency on Dr. T., unfailingly kind, devoted, and knowledgeable as he was. Not only had the medications not brought the promised relief, but the identity of "patient," one who is "sick" and under a doctor's care, only deepened the grooves of self-doubt in my brain, only further devalued my sense of self. I needed to let go of both the belief that something was fundamentally wrong with me and the belief that someone or something outside of myself could fix and save me.

In a subtle way, after each failed drug trial, I had blamed myself. Was I not trying hard enough, not brave enough to tolerate the side effects? But looking back I wonder if my diagnosis: Major Depression, Atypical Depression and Agitated Depression was misleading. Perhaps a more accurate diagnosis would have been Trauma. Perhaps recurring experiences of depression and anxiety were brought on by the underlying cause—trauma and frequent retraumatization. Does the treatment of trauma lend itself to antidepressants? In my case, the answer seemed to be "no."

Perhaps there was an altogether different path to follow.

In the dark of night, I came to a decision. A new intention— which caused an accelerated heartbeat of fear, but excitement as well. I would take my life back into my own hands. I would leap into the void. I would stop taking all anti-depressant medications.

Was this utter folly, or guided inspiration?

I knew I would be running a risk moving away from allopathic medicine, from the care of experts. But the mere thought of taking matters into my own hands brought renewed energy and hope. I felt intrigued and engaged. By discontinuing the ingestion of pharmaceuticals, I would allow my brain to heal. This is the decision I came to that night.

The concept of neuroplasticity pointed to the brain's ability to repair, to form new synaptic connections. Rather than introduce a drug, a foreign substance, I would create the conditions which would allow my nervous system to restore itself. On a conscious level, I did not know that I was working with the effects of trauma. But intuitively, I knew that fixing my fraught nervous system was the correct direction to pursue.

Deep in the night, in those moments of thinking and purpose, I felt the salutary effects of the possibility I was contemplating. I would take a risk. I would forge my own alternative path to healing. As I embraced this decision, sensations of empowerment and strength began to flow into my body.

Creating the conditions for healing was key—what did my physical, emotional, mental, and spiritual self need? What were the optimal conditions that would allow healing to occur? I directed all my efforts to answering these questions. Of course, I had been taking responsibility for seeking answers to these questions for many years. But the years of living with the label "depressive" and waiting for a pharmaceutical cure had slackened my muscles of determination and courage. Now, I felt a new resolve.

INNER CHILD WORK

It was a Mother's Day Sunday. I was in my thirties. My mother, father, and I were eating lunch at a restaurant. My brother was living in Los Angeles at the time, so there was just the three of us.

I had returned to town that morning from my monthly Pathwork weekend gathering.

"I don't understand," I told my parents. "The others in my community seem to become psychologically healthier as we work so hard on our process. Whereas I feel stuck. I try so hard. I don't understand why I am not getting better."

My mother's face turned red, her eyes filled with tears, and she blurted out the following story:

"When you were born, the German doctor sat at my bedside and told me that Jewish people feed their babies too much. I heard a baby crying all the time because my first baby, my boy, died in

Russia. He only lived for thirty days. We hired a nurse for you. She was a German countess who lost everything during the war. She hated Jews. At night, she locked you in your room and would not let us in. She said you should not have feedings at night. She gave you tea and then left you to cry. You lost weight and could not eat. You almost died. I took you to a 'special doctor,' and he gave you a baby formula made of rice.

We sent the nurse away.

You began eating and your cheeks became full and rosy."

"How long did this go on?" I asked.

"Maybe six weeks."

A gloomy, Gothic darkness descended on our table in this crowded suburban restaurant on Mother's Day, this now entirely incongruous setting. Usurped countesses who hate Jews. German doctors. Locked doors at night. The cries of a dying child.

My body reacted to my mother's words—shock, dismay, and something akin to horror. A trauma I was unaware of happened when I was a newborn.

My mother blamed the German doctor and the German "nurse" who hates Jews. Putting the responsibility on the doctor and nurse whom she had invested with so much authority was the way her mind worked. Yet I could see in her face and hear in her voice, she was tormented by guilt. After the initial shock, I timidly asked to know a bit more. My mother's flushed face, her clenched jaw, dark eyes shifting rapidly from side to side—her guilty distress—registered so forcefully upon me that when she didn't reply, I remained silent, and we never spoke of this again.

I wonder if this experience as a newborn—lying alone all night; hungry, cold, wet, my cries weakening into silence, was the cause of the "Empty Universe," sensation I experienced during my darkest moments, feeling trapped in a vast, uncaring, empty space.

Some years later, when I was taking my healing into my own hands, I felt called to experiment with an approach I had read about which suggested that within us, cellularly, lives our wounded child selves. We could access this child self by visualizing every detail of the child's situation, the age of the child, the room or place where the child is, the clothing the child is wearing; every detail bringing the child to life. By breathing deeply and centering ourselves, we could enter the space of the child we once were and emotionally connect with her.

At night, as I lay in my bed, I entered the space of the newborn who had given up on life. I opened the door and saw her lying in her crib. I picked her up and held her tiny body in my arms. I removed her soaked diaper and itchy wool garments, the irritation of the wool felt on my own skin. I put her body in a basin full of warm water and gently sponged off her sour terror. I dried her and wrapped a tiny disposable diaper around her bottom. I dressed her in a soft cotton pink pant and top. I placed a tiny cotton cap on her head. I covered her with a blanket and held her against my beating heart. She was unable to suck. Many nights passed before I felt her readiness to take in a few drops of formula. I held her and rubbed her back, murmuring comforting words.

Every night, for a period of a year or more, I entered this precious space of cellular memory where she lived inside of me. There were difficult nights when she appeared to me gaunt and skeletal, her skin hanging lifeless. But I persevered. I sought to find the place of mercy in me, the source of patience and love, the faith that believed she could heal and become whole.

With the passing of time, she was able to suck, to take in a few mouthfuls of formula, a few inches, a half bottle. Her body's tissues began to fill with nourishment. And as the two of us lay in my bed, it was my adult body, as well as her tiny one, that felt a calming in every cell, a secure falling into warm sleep.

I thought I might try this process, this inner child work, as a restorative healing for the other traumas, for the other little girls, adolescent girls, and even women selves who lived in me.

I turned next to the trauma of the night my daddy was shot. With what trepidation I called up this shattered girl. I was afraid to revisit that night. I needed to call in a helping figure. I invited an angel to come into the house with me. Together, we set up a blue tent in the family living room. We filled the tent with cushions, pillows, and soft blankets. We brought in Diana; thirteen years old. We lit candles with her, placed them on the mantlepiece, each one holding a prayer for Daddy. The loving angel and adult me held Diana in our arms inside the tent, wrapping her shivering body in warm blankets and love. We prayed for Daddy. We sang Psalm 23 for him, "The Lord is My Shepherd." We sang, "Yea, though I walk through the valley of the shadow of death . . . Surely goodness and mercy will follow me all the days of my life and I will dwell in the house of the Lord forever." Over and over, chanting, chanting in English and Hebrew, the language Daddy would recognize. Night after night, thirteen-year-old Diana, adult me, and the Healing Angel. The tent was the holding space, just the right size, our refuge and sanctuary. Inside the tent, my terror eased, my overwrought amygdala, its siren fever pitch, subdued.

I have used this process of corrective repair of traumatic events many times over the years. I go inside to the places where there is a beaten down, hurt me. I visualize and see her in my mind's eye— every detail, what she is wearing, where she is exactly, the room, the place. I enter and let her know I am here, open to hearing how she feels and what she needs. I meet her in every way I feel she can receive. I notice that as I am able to be with her just as she is, she opens up to me more and more. I learn about feelings I had not realized before. I share my adult wisdom with her. I tell her what is true—that even if she made a mistake she is not a bad person. She deserves love and comfort and understanding. When she is hurting, she deserves more love, not less.

HEALING TOUCH

Healing Touch is a therapy that uses gentle hand techniques to re-pattern the person's energy field and accelerate healing of the body, mind, and spirit. This therapy addresses physical, emotional, mental, and spiritual systems, both the corporeal body and the etheric bodies, the quantum level, and the level of beliefs, in order to clear that which no longer serves and to bring about profound healing.

When I studied to become a Healing Touch practitioner, I was awed by the pulsating currents and heat in my hands as they moved around the body, as my hands sensed the chakras and the layers of the auric field. This actual, physical, felt sense in my hands and body as I worked, more than any words spoken, reaffirmed my faith that there is something more, something we name "spiritual." We are not just our physical bodies, we are not just our minds, thoughts, and egos, we are not just our story, our life experiences, and our suffering. There is so much more afoot, even if we don't understand it. This revelation in the form, not of words, but of my own undeniable physical tactile awareness strengthened my spiritual faith and trust in life. And when the time came that I was ready to focus on the awakening process and less on my psychological angst, Healing Touch had already provided me with both entry and indwelling in the non-dual field of consciousness.

FINDING REFUGE

Trauma lives engrained, deeply, in the body, in the very cells of our being; in the nervous system, in our cellular memory, and, it has now been revealed, in our collective and intergenerational memory as well. I found an unexpected, and to me interesting, aspect of trauma healing in finding refuge.

This phenomenon was brought most forcefully upon my awareness one night in San Miguel de Allende. I had spent the late afternoon and early evening with Rachel, her daughter, Stephanie, and Stephanie's little baby boy. During dinner, I told Stephanie about my background as a child of Holocaust survivors.

It had been raining for hours and the night was dark and misty. I felt a sudden urgency to leave Stephanie's home and I inexplicably refused Rachel's offer to phone for a cab nor did I empty my already pressing bladder. Instead, I spoke my hurried goodbyes and dashed from the house. Once out on the empty dark street, I realized I had no idea where I was, nor the direction home. Eventually, I came to a street I recognized which led to a main road. I might have hailed a cab then, but the windows of the few passing cabs were completely fogged, and the drivers could not see me. Nor could I raise my arm to make a motion to be seen. It was as though I was caught up in some implacable force field which compelled me to trudge on. All I wanted to do, or could do, was keep walking, one foot in front of the other, water up past my shins, the cobblestones slick with rain. I climbed higher and higher, up to the neighborhood where I lived.

Finally arriving at my apartment, I was breathing hard and fast, emitting small animal-like whimperings, little screeches of stress and relief, little sighs of pleasure. I peeled off soaked socks and shoes and sopping clothes. I raced around looking for dry towels, lit the propane heater, turned on dim lights. I rubbed my head and body with towels, put on my night shirt and a robe. It was deeply satisfying to arrange my wet shoes and clothes near the heater to dry. I put the kettle on to boil and then with my cup of tea in hand, lowered myself onto the easy chair in front of the *chimenea*. A delicious sense of refuge encompassed me. The comfort I felt is indescribable. I loved the entire experience; meeting the dire straits head on and then finding shelter where I had created warmth and comfort: blessed sanctuary.

This primal story lives in me—danger and refuge, to be repeated over and over. It goes all the way back to Homo sapiens' beginnings, the collective trauma and healing of the cave dweller through to the Holocaust and to being a little refugee girl at Ellis Island. And who knows when else.

I have written the outlines of three novels and let the plot and characters reveal themselves to me in great detail as I take long walks and bike rides. Whether the novel's main character is a male, female, or a child, whether the story takes place in our time or in the 1850's, or even in a post-apocalyptic future—the underlying theme is always the same. The characters face hardships, even tragedies—losing parents, pogroms, slavery, loneliness, abusive husbands, betrayal, escape from authoritarian brave new worlds—as they journey to Home, create home, create safety, shelter. A physical home. A community. Refuge. Homecoming.

The latest novel I have "written" could become five or more interlocking novels, involving many characters. The story of these characters' lives have kept me company for years. They tell me their story—and each time I feel a soothing warmth, comfort, and even transcendence.

Anna, a toddler wearing a yellow silk dress, an ermine cape and a gold heart locket is walking in town holding her nanny's hand, when a man on horseback grabs her and speeds away with her. He takes her to his Romany encampment and gives her to his wife, who is childless. The wife is a loving, kind mother but she dies when Anna is fifteen years old. Within the year, the "grandmother" is dying as well. She tells Anna it is no longer safe for her to remain in the encampment. Her destiny and fate lie elsewhere, but in order to meet her destiny, she must undertake a challenging journey.

Anna, fifteen years old, disguised as a boy, carrying a heavy pack and rolled silk rug, waits until night, when the Romany encampment is quiet. She exits the caravan and with her dog, Chaika, at her side, makes her way to the open road. For two months, she treks in a westerly direction carrying the heavy rucksack, the rolled silk carpet attached to its bottom. On her way from somewhere in eastern Europe, she walks and walks. Sometimes the driver of a wagon carrying his wife, children, and a grandma offers her a ride, and she climbs on. Two months into her journey, the spirit of the woman she called "Grandmother" guides her to leave the westerly road and head south. Another month passes.

Now she feels it. One late afternoon, it is time to turn off the road. To leave the main road: so difficult to trust this intuitive sense. She turns left and a ways down she sees cultivation, fruit trees, a stream. She comes upon an outhouse, a tool shed, a garden nearly parched for lack of water, and a small white house. Anna approaches cautiously. She knocks on the door several times. When no one answers, she tries the door handle and opens the door. Inside the house, there is a table and on the table a note:

If you have made your way here and want
to make this your home, it is yours.

Blessings,
Aaron

Anna walks over to the well and fills the bucket. Walking to and from the garden, she refills the bucket many times, soaking the parched earth. That is the first order of business, the vegetable garden. She sits on the bench in front of the house, eats bread, cheese, and sausage from her rucksack. She walks into the house and bolts the door from the inside. She lays down her pack and the heavy rug. Chaika lies on the floor beside her. She removes her socks and boots. Shelter, quiet, four walls, a bolted door—for the first time in three months, she can drop into a protected sleep of oblivion, held by walls that surround her.

And my own body, along with Anna's, settles, feeling that exquisite release deep in every cell. I relive the moments of Anna's arrival, and the weeks that follow as she secures her homestead. I relive these delectable moments over and over and over again.

I cleave to my home, to my novels, to my imagination.

As I ready for bed, I feel the walls of my home embracing me. I feel the safety, the deep healing occurring. Home, the order and peace of home, profound refuge.

CHAPTER 14

Inside the
Trauma Body

ALONE, WALKING HOME FROM SCHOOL the day the bullying trauma began, I experienced fear so intense, it was as though
I had stuck my finger into an electric socket. An explosive current
hurled sparks of terror throughout my nervous system.

When Sandy broke his arm on my thirteenth birthday—that
current struck again. From that day on, I lived within a nervous
system and a belief that I am at fault, bad, and blameworthy. There
had been a sea change within my body, my mind, and my emotions. My identity was altered.

Then, seven months later, my father was shot. My nervous
system was already compromised, already primed for terror. The
night of the shooting, this terror became so acute it jammed the
thermostat regulating fear responses in my body. My amygdala
was now frozen, permanently set to high alert.

My fearless ice skater's body had devolved into a body of fear.

It became my lifelong task and responsibility to work with this trauma body as it presents itself in each moment.

Each morning, the moment I wake from my sleep state, the stress hormone cortisol pours into my belly. In the very same seconds my self is waking up, orienting, and remembering who I am— painful knots of fear are already present in my torso. My diaphragm is a tight band of pain. My mind, now engaged, identifying with the signals coming from my body, scans the scene, searching for what is amiss. Default neural pathways are triggered, sending thoughts matching the clenching gut, thoughts about what is bad and wrong with me and my life. A negative feedback loop is rolling.

Thus begins a subtle, semi-conscious, and pernicious process. My mind attacks and blames my self. My mind believes the discomfort in my body is my fault. There is a turning on the self, a continual and persistent self-rejection.

My work is to make this process conscious, to become aware of self-rejection as it is happening and to bring love and self-acceptance to this suffering.

Every day for decades, for some or most or all of the day, I experienced symptoms of depression and anxiety. I did not have knowledge of retraumatization or dysregulation. Instead, I thought of myself as neurotic and depressed. I felt shame. Shame dwelt just below the level of consciousness, always present, determining my sense of who I was in each moment.

My trauma-damaged body, characterized by fear and dread, telegraphed messages to my mind and emotions. Thousands of triggers shared an underlying theme, a root cause—the threat was that someone was blaming or devaluing me, telling me I had done something wrong. And I was blaming and devaluing myself.

I did not have a platform within myself on which to stand to weather these onslaughts. There was no presence living within me able to hold my goodness and worth and mirror it back to me. No supportive voice within could help me and believe in me.

Instead, when a painful or devaluing interaction occurred, I would tumble into a retraumatization reaction in the body. Racing thoughts, perseverating thoughts. Shame. Nausea. Pervasive dread like a vapor within and around me. Buzzing terror as if every molecule was on fire. A weight of dismay on my chest. A hollowed out, imploded collapse in my middle. Clenching painful guts, like twisted towels, every drop of moisture squeezed out of them.

My trauma body was a small, constricted, tightly bound vessel. My body had difficulty holding and containing any strong physical or emotional charge, whether pleasure or pain. Energy needed to be discharged to bring me back to stasis, the narrow stasis which I could tolerate.

Talking was a way to tame the wild currents coursing through me. I talked to my mother. She was kind enough to listen, to keep track of the characters in my tales, to tolerate the unstoppable flood of words pouring into her ear through the telephone. My phone calls and words also served her—to stem her feelings of loneliness, to give her a feeling of connection with me, even to entertain her. But the talking could be destructive for me. Often, after pouring myself out, I felt heightened anxiety. I lost all sense of boundaries. I felt empty, as though I had given myself away.

Or I imposed my talking on others, oblivious of their feelings. My son was one captive audience, especially when we were in the car together, especially when we were driving on the freeway, when the anxiety in my body ramped up several notches. I could not give myself an accounting of what was happening, that I was driving him crazy with the incessant discharging of my fears, as one worry after another surfaced. He would finally erupt, and I never knew what hit me. I did not mean to hurt him or cause distress or harm. I was doing what I was compelled to do. Yet, deep inside, a part of me knew. I tried to rein myself in—but the energetic charge of fear coursing through me was stronger than my resolve.

Joy, happiness, and excitement were challenging as well. Sometimes the emotional charge of these powerful energies would overwhelm me.

I would phone someone the minute something good happened. I told myself I wanted to share my happiness, but really I needed to discharge energy by talking, to achieve a level I could tolerate.

Or, *in extremis,* I would have an accident and that would stop the flow of good feelings altogether.

Like when my brother and sister-in-law visited me in my city, San Miguel de Allende, my happy place in the highlands of Mexico. I was so excited and happy to see them, that within twenty minutes of our meeting, I fell flat on my face on the cobblestones, blood flowing from my forehead, nose, and cheeks.

Or the first year I returned from San Miguel de Allende, elated with the discovery of this beautiful place—I slipped on the ice the following morning. My elbow required surgery—a plate, six pins— and bike riding suspended until the end of summer.

Or the year I was finally free of an orthopedic boot I had been wearing for months. I walked around San Miguel in my regular shoes so happy and free—until that same night, when I lost my orientation in the bathroom of my new apartment—and fell back-wards over a tile ledge into the shower, causing a foot injury that lasted for months.

I had an ambivalent relationship to pleasure. My system was better able to tolerate it when the pleasure was braided with pain. I felt ecstatic pleasure with Uri. This was acceptable because the relationship was held in a space of uncertainty, arrivals, and departures—pleasure laced with pain.

I devoted myself to finding ways to ease the suffering of living in my trauma body. There was my body, there was my mind, and there was a "feeling me" who was trapped inside this challenged body. "I" wanted and needed to save and rescue "her."

I found nature to be a potent healer. Bike riding and walking in nature became my most powerful line of defense. I jumped out of bed in the morning and hopped on my bike, riding as fast and as far as I could. I created a 17-mile route, a bike ride to beauty. It was so simple, this gift to myself, so simple and profound. My life opened to the caresses of sweet morning air on my cheeks, opened to glory, to the holy of holies—to a ride gliding under a canopy of fully grown trees. I arrived at a lake and found a favorite bench where I watched the ducks, occasional herons, and swans. Standing on a bridge, I visited a waterfall and if I kept my gaze on the river flowing underneath I could shut out the traffic noise and imagine Tom Sawyer and Huckleberry Finn, heading down to the creek to fish. On the return route, I rode down and then up a steep hill, the green filling me, the sight of the woods, hiking paths, and a small wetland with fuchsia-colored lily pads flying past—a thrill each morning.

Day after day, no matter how many times I rode this route, I felt pleasure, joy, and strength. I rejoiced in the act of bringing goodness and wellbeing to my self. I rebuilt my identity a little bit each day—coming to embody a self who feels pleasure, who lives well.

I sought a healing path. I came to believe, to know, and to trust with all my heart and mind, that it is possible for the mind to rewire and heal the brain. I came to know, to trust, and to believe with all my heart and soul, that "underneath" trauma, my natural state is one of peace and stillness.

I experienced moments of transcendence.

I woke one summer morning, familiar dread creeping up my torso. I observed the physical sensations of dis-ease that arose and watched dark thoughts seeking to insinuate themselves into the forefront of my mind. I saw the attack coming, and on this particular morning, identifying the thinking process helped me not to be at its mercy.

I practiced opening my awareness to the sweet stillness in the room, the leaves on the trees, framed in the skylight in the sloped ceiling across from my bed.

I became aware of the mellow light refracting off the crystals of the chandelier which hangs above the staircase, a campy relic from the dining room of the house I grew up in. My eyes moved to the cheer of the red-apple-colored frame surrounding the Chinese print on the far wall, depicting women bent over rice paddies, their brightly colored Mao jackets center stage.

My attention shifted from the seeming solidity of my body to a felt Presence, a quality of modest thickening of the air in the room. It was as though my body began to dissolve, larger and larger spaces arising between each cell, all merging into Awareness. The thickening of the energy field made itself known by an ever so slight and gentle nudging sensation into which I merged.

As I grow older, I live summer with a fierce cherishing, knowing I can no longer count on endless summers ahead. The recognition of time passing merges with a growing aptitude for unalloyed, appreciative joy, as though there is, after all, all the time in the world. Or more likely, no time but the timeless One Time—lush, exquisite summer to which I surrender.

But since the threat to our democracy, since the mass shootings recurring and accelerating, since the more pronounced ecological ravages to Mother Earth, since Covid, since the war in Ukraine— my ability to inhabit the non-dual space has been challenged. My sense of security has felt threatened, the ground eroding beneath my feet. My sense of refuge is disturbed; my mind in a mad scramble seeking safety.

Whether I can manifest healing, peace, and stillness in a sustained way or whether I fall back into re-traumatization in my body/mind, whether I experience moments of blessed peace or I feel trapped in fear and dread—I embrace my overriding task—to provide a refuge within myself of unconditional love—however my body/mind is expressing herself in any given moment.

This question emerges. How do we heal trauma when our collective trauma is becoming more dire?

And for me personally: how do I hold and live with the indigestible, the intergenerational trauma I carry as a child of survivors?

CHAPTER 15

A Child of Survivors

HOUSEHOLD NAMES WHEN I WAS growing up.

Hitler.

Stalin.

They were part of the landscape, they lived under our roof—in the rooms, in the memories, in the heartbreak, in the indescribable losses.

Not only their deeds but they—they themselves—loomed over us.

One evening, as I pulled into my driveway, the dark and bitter cold pressed an air of desolation upon me. The car radio was tuned to the local public radio station and my attention was drawn to a broadcast in progress. Anne Applebaum was giving an interview about her latest book, *Red Famine, Stalin's War on Ukraine*. The relevance of her words seeped into my awareness as I sat in the car listening. The heater blew blasts of warm air onto my face and legs, yet I felt chilled through, penetrated by the bitter cold, the gloomy darkness, and the unfolding tragedy revealed by Applebaum's words.

Her research had uncovered that the starvation my mother lived through as a young girl in Odessa was not due to a natural catastrophe but was diabolically engineered by Stalin, the revered leader. My mother had told me stories about that time: my grandmother waiting in line for hours to buy a loaf of bread, my mother's hunger and tears, the malnutrition sores covering her body. Three million, nine hundred thousand people in the Ukraine starved to death between 1932-1933, when my mother was twelve years old, and her brother Saul/Soolinka was ten.

Thankfully, my deceased mother would never know the starvation she had endured as a young girl was the result of Stalin's intentional acts. But what I did not understand was that hearing the grave truths Anne Applebaum had uncovered in her research and was now revealing, reactivated the trauma I carry in my body, the trauma of being a child of survivors.

Nor had I understood, when I read Arthur Koestler's book *Darkness at Noon* as a teenager, that the book would have an indelible impact upon me. Grayness engulfed me as I read, the gray walls of the prison, the gray prison uniforms, the gray faces of the prisoners. Reading the book, a deep inward fear about the up is down and black is white insanity of totalitarianism spread throughout my body. People were squashed brutally, without mercy. It did not matter that the men undergoing extreme mental torture had been Stalin's *"tovarichi"*—his comrades. The leader had supreme power and if he wanted his former comrades to confess to crimes they did not commit, if he wanted to disgrace them publicly and then execute them—he could do it. These were the infamous Stalin Purge Trials of 1937. Millions of people were sent to the Gulag or executed because one man had total power in this totalitarian system of government that was the U.S.S.R.

The twisted injustice of this system became part of the lived sense of my body.

My mother told me about that time of terror: of teachers disappearing from one day to the next, textbooks replaced with different versions of the "truth," hearts pounding nightly from the dread of the knock on the door, the secret police, come to round up innocent people, her father among them. He was one of the lucky ones, returning home after thirty days, pale and thin.

Years before the Holocaust, before the escape from the Nazis, before the murder of her brother and the death of her fiancé in the Nazi invasion of Russia in WWII—before all of this, my mother was already traumatized.

From the time I was a young girl, I had listened to my mother's stories. I absorbed her pain, but I did not understand until years later that my mother's suffering had also traumatized me.

". . .intergenerational trauma refers to the effects of serious untreated trauma that has been experienced by one or more members of a family, group, or community and has been passed down from one generation to the next through epigenetic factors . . ."

—Thomas Hubl, *Healing Collective Trauma.*

And then, of course, there is Hitler.

I cannot remember being a child who did not know about Hitler and the Holocaust. I do not have a memory of finding out. Rather my sense of myself, my identity, is of one who has always known.

I have no memory of a life free of Hitler.

When I was thirteen years old, I read the book *Exodus* by Leon Uris. In it there are graphic details of the concentration camps. I did not have nightmares after reading the book. Instead, I sunk into a visceral knowing of the cruelty of which people are capable. The strong impression was not of evil per se, not an abstract word like "evil"— rather that one person, facing another, could act with heartless cruelty and indifference. That is what seared me— the intense suffering of another did not move the perpetrators. They were not affected. There was nothing I could do about this, it had already happened, it was possible in this world. I felt as though I was living in a malevolent universe. I felt there was no escape.

There was the surface life and the subterranean one. On the surface, the sun shone down on our peaceful suburb outside of Detroit, Michigan. Neat houses and tended lawns, a library, a community center, a skating rink, an excellent school system. It was like living in a Hollywood musical. At any moment, the people on the street might burst into song and dance across the perfect green lawns, tapping up and down the porch stairs and twirling around the banisters. While way down below, where only I could see, there were gray prison cells with one bulb burning all night, prisoners questioned and denied sleep until they broke and signed bogus confessions. There were naked young women, heads shaven, hands and arms covering their modesty as their captors forced them into the showers and turned on the gas. I could see them; I could enter their bodies and feel their nakedness. I choked from the gas fumes. It was disloyal not to accompany them.

As the years passed, I became impatient with myself. "The War is Over," I would say. This came to me as startling news. "The War is Over; it ended many years ago." I repeated the phrase again and again, "The War is Over, The War is Over." What I did not understand, what I could not offer to myself with kindness, was that the war was over—but the trauma it had inflicted lived on.

The Holocaust bleeds through in strange moments:

I walk down the street when suddenly I hear footsteps alongside me. I have become a bystander, as a column of Jews; men, women, children, the elderly, dressed in layers, fur coats or best wool, carrying the one allotted suitcase, walk next to me in an orderly procession. Their neighbors stand by, some sympathetic, some jeering or spitting. The Jews walk with dignity to the trains, to the waiting cattle cars.

Or I sit in a synagogue watching a program the children, my son among them, have prepared for a holiday. The door to the sanctuary opens and my daddy's parents, brothers and sisters, their spouses and children, file in. They sit down in the pew alongside me, figures in black and white. They fill the pews, the entire lot of them; finally they have arrived, and I am not sitting alone anymore.

These reveries come suddenly, unbidden. It is as though someone has drawn back a curtain and the setting for an entirely different scene is revealed, one that had always been there but was camouflaged by the scene of normalcy.

My mother spoke often of "home," of her life before the war. Always the death of her brother was part of the telling. And without fail, even thirty, forty or fifty years after the event, she cried when she told me about the night before they left Russia. She and her parents needed to tear up anything in their possession with Russian writing on it. And that night they tore up the last letter Soolinka wrote, the one from the hospital where he lay dying, the one with his blood on it.

A surviving photograph of Soolinka in a silver frame has prominence on a bookshelf in my bedroom. When I walk up the stairs to my bedroom at night and turn the corner onto the landing,

Soolinka's face looks out at me, his penetrating eyes burrowing into my heart.

I do not know when I learned his death was a murder. My mother told me about his letters home from the front, where he described the intense, unremitting, crude, and ingrained anti-Semitism of his fellow Russian compatriots. He wrote that if he survived the war, he would go to Palestine. My mother, who had been a Young Pioneer and was proud to wear the red kerchief, was shocked by her brother's writings. Palestine?

Soolinka was shot in the back by his own troops, and he died of his wounds at the age of nineteen. I climb the stairs and round the corner and there he is. Tears and sometimes sobs escape me. Maybe it would be better not to display Soolinka's photo. Maybe I should hide him in a drawer.

One day, I came upstairs to retrieve something from my closet. I tried to stay on the surface, to continue with my mundane tasks, to remain in the here and now. But sobs surfaced in my chest and emerged from my throat—when I heard these words, Soolinka's words, in my heart: "Don't cry," he says, "We are well now."

There is scientific research, a field named epigenetics, which describes the physical effects of trauma on the second generation of Holocaust survivors. Cortisol levels have been assessed, disturbances in the expression of genes have been studied. It is helpful to know that physical effects of trauma on the second generation are measurable. But what concerns me are those moments when something stimulates the place of horror within me, an unexpected stimulus—and my entire being is wrenched, as if the Holocaust in its full savagery has entered my awareness for the first time. I feel stricken, unsure how I can go on.

Yet, somehow, I have made a place for this undigestible massive occurrence. I have learned to live with it.

The feelings I had as a child of survivors added to the wounds to my self concept caused by the other four traumas. I was different, marked by tragedy.

I wanted to heal, to become like others, to be more lighthearted, to put the Holocaust aside and have a more benign view of the world. I denied myself the compassion and understanding I needed. My self-blame was self-betrayal.

Myra Goodman, the co-author of the book *Quest for Eternal Sunshine: A Holocast Survivor's Journey from Dark to Light*, wrote: "It's taken me decades, but I've recently begun to recognize that much of my fear and sadness are rarely all me or mine. . . While it's impossible for me to escape my legacy as a daughter of two Holocaust survivors, there is a powerful liberation in discovering that my intense emotions and fearful thought patterns have far-reaching roots. This awareness helps me break free from self-criticism and put to rest old beliefs about being hopelessly neurotic."

I have wondered what my life would have been had the traumas of Hitler and Stalin been the "only" traumas I carried. What if the traumas I experienced in my first year of life and from ages eleven to thirteen had not happened? Would I have been an equally traumatized person?

When I am reactivated by trauma in my daily life, it is most often due to the effects of the bullying, the blame when Sandy broke his arm, the devaluing of my worth and the effects of those on my body—rather than the reality of the Holocaust.

It is my belief that if second generation trauma was the "only" major trauma I endured, the damage to the core of my identity and the damage to my body's nervous system would not have occurred. I would have become the adult version of the skater girl I once was.

I had been focusing my energies on my spiritual quest. I was studying, teaching, practicing, and immersing myself in non-dual consciousness. My toes and even a foot stood in the waters of the awakened state. The ego was loosening its grip. Life was revealing a possibility of spaciousness. Years of effort were bearing fruit into non-effort.

And then came the summer of 2016 when I rode my bike along my seventeen-mile route, the houses and lawns bigger and grander as I approached Quarton Lake. As I rode under majestic trees and blue skies, the joy I often felt was marred by Trump lawn signs and Hillary behind bars signs nailed onto trees, more of them in this area of town than I would have expected.

That summer, on a late Sunday afternoon, I was invited to dinner at my brother's house. We sat outside on the deck, salmon cooking on the grill. "I think Trump might win," I said. "An unease is growing in me."

"You are so negative," my brother hurled at me.

In that moment, several layers of truth were floating in the air between my brother and me. There was his annoyed put-down, the message that I and my reality are wrong. In this instance, my premonition was correct, but my brother was onto something. When I am in a re-traumatized state, my presence can weigh heavily on others, and he had been the recipient of this many times. I do tend to impose the cacophony of trauma voices within me, to burden those around me with the dramas and fears *du jour*. I can miss the joy of summer worrying about the election in the autumn.

This was the confounding truth.

And there was more.

It is true that trauma attacks the core of one's identity. In order to heal, I needed to reclaim myself. I had lived my life as a bad person trying to be good. I needed to claim my ordinary ok-ness. I needed to trust my perceptions. I was at times too negative, but I was also often spot on. Maybe my reality was distorted by the Holocaust, but it was also informed by the Holocaust. I am a student of history, a student of human nature, with years of experience as a psychotherapist. Maybe the wise me was the canary in the coal mine.

After the election, came the frequent references to Putin. Had the Russians undermined the election process? What were they doing playing a role in our country? Sinister sensations swirled in my body. Trump campaign people involved with Russian oligarchs, involved with Russian operatives—the nightly broadcasts were full of such news.

The Nazi rally in Charlottesville: "very fine people on both sides." The Helsinki meeting between Trump and Putin, the phone call with Zelensky. Alexander Vindman and his brother unceremoniously led out of government buildings, dismissed from their jobs. "This is America, here right matters," Vindman said. I hope so, but are you sure? Too many foreign policy decisions which aided Putin rather than the U.S.—the NATO alliance maligned, our backs turned on our European allies, our abandonment of the Kurds paving the way for Putin in Syria—on and on.

All this so reminiscent, so familiar. "Autocracy, Fascism," words newly referenced in interviews, in op-ed pieces, in nightly news broadcasts. Yet, these words had been with me as long as I could remember.

War in Ukraine. Putin, the fascist, the dictator, the totalitarian KGB agent, is fighting the war "to rid Ukraine of the Nazis" he says. He wants to self-cleanse Russia from "the vermin and traitors" who are not going along with his "special operation." Stalin's Purge Trials are referenced on the front page of the New York Times.

Volodymyr Yermolenko, a Ukrainian philosopher, captured the essence of this moment. He referred to the famed Russian author

Fyodor Dostoyevsky and his book, *Crime and Punishment.* "Russia is a nation," Yermolenko said, "of crime without punishment and punishment without crime."

Putin and Stalin's evil acts have merged—old and ongoing trauma coming full circle.

Soolinka

CHAPTER 16

Breaking the Spell

*T*HIS IS THE APOTHEOSIS.

Here the pieces of the puzzle fall into place.

Now we have come to the heart of the matter—to breaking the spell.

It was never true—the Bad Me.

I had internalized the negative projections of others.

I am wearing my headphones, talking on the phone as I ride my bike. In our conversation, I am being told I am at fault, what I said was wrong. My caller is telling me *you always do it.* Listening to his voice and words, the familiar implosion begins. Pressured tears behind my eyes, the collapse in my middle, terror, dread, the pounding heart, the clanging of danger—losing altitude, as in an elevator, cables broken, rushing to the bottom, to an obliterating crash.

After this phone conversation, I stop riding. I straddle my bike by the side of the road and phone my friend Brian.

I caught re-traumatization as it was occurring.

Brian explains this is a negative projection. My caller is feeling guilty about what he did and cannot own it. He is projecting his feeling of badness on me. That is what is happening. That is all that is happening. I am not in danger, whatever my caller says or thinks. The signals I receive from my body are trauma responses, not reality. My pounding heart quiets.

"Brian, you have known me for over forty years. Do you think I am bad?" "No," says Brian. "I don't think you are bad. You are a wonderful woman."

I have never heard Brian's voice so husky, warm, and loving.

I believe him.

But before? Weeks and months of my life were eaten up and lost in the aftermath of occurrences such as these.

One balmy late summer afternoon, on a restaurant's outdoor terrace, I sat at a table with friends. These cherished friends, a couple, invited me to meet for lunch. They wanted, they said, to hear my thoughts and insights regarding an occurrence in their family.

It seemed to me the situation they described hearkened back to a pattern established in their lives many years ago. A taboo, enforced silence, surrounded this pattern. But much healing had occurred. I naively believed it was safe to speak of this now. I expressed what had never been allowed to be said. I knew what I said was true. But my friend was outraged. Perhaps I had gone too far.

In the days and weeks that followed, I wrote voluminous emails explaining and apologizing. I was distraught. Obsessed. Consumed. Nothing of me was left over for everyday tasks or concerns about my appearance. I wore the same black pants and black shirt every day. Wash wear, wash wear. They thought I was bad, and I was afraid I was. Internal dialogues with them looped endlessly in my head.

I sat in my car in the parking lot at Trader Joe's. The door was propped open to let in a light breeze. The husband of the couple, a dear pillar of my life, was letting me know in our phone conversation, that because of what I had said, the friendship was in jeopardy. He felt protective of his wife. I had upset her, what I said was uncalled for. I broke into a cold sweat, felt faint with nauseous dread. It was not only that the friendship may end, but worse: the friendship would end because of my badness.

Brian witnessed me going through this ordeal. He told me: "Other people let peoples' words go right through them. They hold on to their own truths. But you have a shelf inside of yourself and the words of others land there. You internalize the negative projections of others. You don't stay with what you know, what your truth is, instead you take on theirs."

"*Internalize the negative projection.*" I had not heard the term before. I tried to feel into its meaning. People are afraid of their emotional pain, so they project blame onto others.

After considering Brian's words, I saw the incident with new eyes. I had spoken truths the wife, my friend, was not ready to face. She could not admit her feelings of guilt and shame. Would that I had been a healthier, more intact person, one who knew it was sufficient to say: "I am sorry my words hurt you. Hurting you was not my intention." Then allow the matter rest, to leave her to choose whether to work with her painful feelings or not.

The friendship with these dear ones weathered the storm and endured. And—I learned a valuable lesson.

Recently, I read a passage in a book which alluded to this phenomenon: "Wouldn't it be incredible if everyone could be purged, somehow, of the projected not-them badness that they internalized and perhaps have acted out because their souls have been so damaged?" *In the Body of the World,* Eve Ensler.

Dr. Gabor Maté, a trauma specialist and trauma survivor, describes trauma as an overwhelming threat with which one cannot cope. Trauma is not only what happens to us, but what happens inside of us as a result of what happened.

Trauma attacks the core of a person's identity.

I was bad for being my birth father's daughter. I was cruelly bullied those last six weeks of sixth grade—scapegoated and rejected. I internalized Eva's betrayal and Jeffrey's cruelty. I was to blame and condemned for Sandy breaking his arm. Gun violence tore my nervous system to shreds. The men I loved or married were blamers of the first order, externalizers, and negative projectors. I nearly went to the psych ward after listening to Uri yell on the phone about my badness. He hung up on me and I thought I would never see him again. When he showed up several days later it was as though nothing had happened. I wondered who was crazy, him or me. I was a ball and chain on Irv's leg, to blame for not becoming religious, for not seeing the truth of his path. And I was always wrong and to blame when I tried to tell my mother her words hurt me.

I see it all now. I see how it unfolded.

When I returned to the United States from Israel, I encountered the Pathwork.

"The Pathwork is a body of practical spiritual wisdom that lays out a step-by-step journey into personal transformation and wholeness down to the very core of our being, offering guidance and advice for self-development and personal growth. It is a voyage of discovery to the Real Self through the layers of our defense, denial, and fear."

The first Pathwork meeting I attended was a process group. Frank, my colleague from work who introduced me to the Pathwork, took the floor. His voice and delivery were sincere. There were no false notes. He spoke simply, exposing that which we conceal from one another. He spoke of his feelings of insecurity, of envy, of inferiority, of aggressive impulses towards those in the group he believed were "better than him" or who might have thought they were his superiors. He was voicing feelings, I realized, that often live within us, the eternal hum when we relate to one another. He was exposing the underbelly of our social interactions—the thoughts and feelings we do not say aloud or admit, which we instead act out in endless games of posturing, competing, and one-upmanship.

So this is how it's done, I thought: remove the social masks we wear, share our true feelings, the ones we hide from one another, take responsibility for what lives within us. Impeccable emotional honesty. Encounter one another from the heart of our authentic selves.

The Pathwork teachings pointed to a possible way home for humanity, for our poor benighted species. If we looked deeply into ourselves, I thought, and owned everything, there would be nothing left to defend or hide. If we chose to face our pain, move through and release it, we would not need to project our painful feelings onto others. If the layers of our defense and conditioning were no longer our shields, clutched to our chests for dear life—our True Nature, the seed of the Divine within us, would transform ourselves and the world.

However, even in the Pathwork community, the outcomes were uneven. Some Pathworkers were impeccable, beacons of inspiration and love. With others, I experienced disappointment and disillusion. This was the most painful and disheartening of all. I had to accept that many of us humans, perhaps most, are stuck in our conditioning and fear.

I moved on from active involvement in the Pathwork community. I went on to practice mindfulness meditation. I studied Buddhism. I immersed myself in non-dual consciousness teachings. Yet the wisdom in the Pathwork lectures and the courageous healing work we did together remained woven into the fabric of my being.

In my work with clients in my psychotherapy practice—I presumed I had their permission to look behind the mask. They said they wanted to feel better. Yet some fought hard to protect their defenses—to blame others for their problems. I sought to reassure them. We are all the same inside. We all struggle with the same fears and misconceptions.

This is the human condition: the personal, the social and the political.

The Germans, after losing WWI, could not tolerate their pain and humiliation. They would not take responsibility for their aggressive, militaristic culture, which led them into war and defeat. Instead, they projected their shame—they scapegoated. They held rallies of mass delusion. They convinced themselves the Communists and the Jews were the cause of their problems. The solution was to eradicate the Jews and Communists and homosexuals and disabled from the earth. All this because the Germans could not and would not tolerate feelings of emotional pain, of defeat, and self-doubt.

Donald Trump could never be a loser. Everyone else was a "loser," but not him, not Donald. So he did not lose the election. The election was stolen from him. For Donald, a threat to his ego is unbearable. He would rather tear our nation apart.

Putin, the KGB agent from the powerful Soviet Union, was a positive identity that could offset the pain of the straitened circumstances of his childhood. But the Soviet Union and its empire collapsed. This was unendurable. He must set this right. Every life lost or life upended in Russia's war on Ukraine is a direct result of one man's inability or unwillingness to tolerate his emotional pain, to tolerate and work with feelings of ego diminishment and humiliation.

We, as the human collective, are faced with this challenge now—to work through our personal, intergenerational and collective traumas by learning to meet our inner experience with understanding and compassion. We are called on to choose vulnerability and self-reflection over denial and projecting our pain onto others, to choose self-responsibility rather than blame, to face our emotional pain rather than act out in destructive ways. As a species we are called to this next step in the evolution of consciousness. Our survival depends on it.

CHAPTER 17

Rebuilding the Self

THROUGHOUT THE YEARS, WHEN YET another healing opportunity presented itself—whether it was the Pathwork, Healing Touch, anti-depressant medications, mindfulness meditation, inner child work, non-dual consciousness, and more—hope for a full recovery would arise eternal in my heart. Each time, I believed I would overcome the painful loop of trauma thinking and trauma body. Each time I thought I would, at last, function on a level playing field—able to use my energy, creativity, and inner resources for living rather than leaking energy, siphoned off to manage inner turmoil and distress. Each time I believed my struggles would cease and be replaced by inner stillness.

The expectation for a full recovery, after years of disappointment, was perhaps naïve. Yet I strove never to relinquish it. And I was uplifted by the reassurance that other than the anti-depressant medications, all my efforts, all discoveries and breakthroughs, did bring me along the path to healing. But none ushered in a full stop to the dysregulation of trauma which plagued me.

With the breaking of the spell I thought I would finally be set free.

But even that was not enough. More was required.

After learning I had been internalizing the negative projections of others for a lifetime, I sought to correct my wrong perceptions and teach myself basic truths. The most fundamental truth was—I am not "bad," no matter what others say and do. My psychological safety does not reside with the other. But as much as I told myself this fundamental truth, my body and my brain's entrenched neural pathways were not in accord. The well-worn grooves in my brain believing me to be Bad continued firing, and I fell back into the traumatized state again and again.

And then a bit of guidance encouraged me into a hitherto un-planned direction. It started when I read it takes forty-five days for a new neural pathway to be established in the brain. A fledgling neu-ral pathway emerges as the old, well-worn one begins the process of withering and falling into disuse.

But how is this done?

The promise of building a new neural path in forty-five days did not come with an instruction manual. It was up to me to craft my own method for building a new neural net.

One day when riding my bike, I became very stern with myself.

I asked myself what I could absolutely, positively, assert to be the case about who and what I am.

Declaring "I am good" did not ring true. "I am good, not bad"—I just didn't believe it.

So what could I state to be impeccably and forcefully accurate?

"I am a worthwhile person."

Yes.

This attestation felt solid and held steady.

"I am a worthwhile person."

This I can affirm. It is so.

What other claim could I make and stand behind 100%?
"I have character defects and make mistakes.
My flaws are not worse than the flaws of others. Nor am I better than others."
This new understanding was revolutionary. For deep within me, so embedded I did not consciously know I felt this, I believed my flaws and character defects were outside of the continuum of normal. And now, somehow, I had arrived at the truth—"my flaws are not worse than other peoples."
This new awareness was unaccountably freeing. It brought forth a profound sigh of release.
Simple, ordinary flaws and frailties.
I gave myself permission to be human, to become a member of the human family.

I visualized a sparkly cascade, a net of tiny stars flowing along luxuriant quantities of webbing in my brain. A beautiful healing field.

Daily, during my morning meditation, I initiated a healing practice. I reviewed each assertion of self-worth. I felt into its veracity and its power. I felt its solidity, the way it rang true in my body.
I revisited the true concepts several times throughout the day—"I am a worthwhile person; my character flaws are no better or worse than anyone else's."
Checking in, validating, reaffirming.
Visualizing the sparkling cascade of neurons.
Practicing.

The challenge would be if I could bring this work to bear during moments of threat—when I experienced anxiety and the trauma body quaked, when the old bad thoughts pressed upon me from within, or when a negative projection came flying in my direction. Those moments, when the old sinking feeling began, would be my opportunity to bring forth the new self-concepts and test their veracity. Do I believe I am a worthwhile person? Yes, this is irrefutable. Do I have permission to have character flaws just like any other person, no better and no worse? Yes, permission is granted.

By affirming these truths again and again—I held firm.

Abiding on this earth became a subtly different experience. I was cautious, of course—after all this time and effort, after the many disappointments—could this evolving shift be trusted? A heavy mantle seemed to lift from my shoulders. Less fear, more confidence, a growing ease. A lightness of being. Sheltered within the depth of my emotional body I found a place of refuge—the dwelling place of abiding self-love and self-acceptance.

Welcoming myself into the human family, knowing myself as worthy, heralded in a reckoning with my first father—if I am no longer bad—then neither is he.

A lifetime has passed.

I am a one year old baby—shocked by his absence.

I am an eleven year old girl—shocked by his sudden appearance in my life, by learning the details of his perfidy.

I am the adolescent girl—dismayed by my mother's need to malign him. Knowing too much—and too little—about him.

I am the bike-riding woman—grateful for this gift he has bequeathed me, sensing our kinship.

I am an older woman, whose son has more years than my first father. I feel both maternal tenderness towards him, and want to reprimand him for his behavior.

I grieve the tragedy of his untimely death.

My heart opens and closes and opens again.

I embrace a more fulsome compassion for us all—for our flawed, halting humanness. For the pain we cause those whom we love the most as we rub against the unhealed parts of ourselves and each other. This is the human story here on planet earth, the way of the world.

CHAPTER 18

Überleben

I LAUGH WHEN I REMEMBER THE sly grin on my mother's face as she uttered Yiddish maxims. Her leaving me with these Yiddishisms is so ironic—she had always held a rather snobbish attitude towards the language and the people who spoke it. They were the common folk, not sophisticated like her own Russian-speaking background. In fact, I never heard her carry on a conversation in the folk language, and I wonder if she could have. But here she is, coming up with pithy Yiddish phrases for all occasions.

"*Ein mool in a Yoivel,*" she would say when she thought a hope or expectation of mine was unrealistic. "It happens once in a Jubilee."

Or when I complained of someone's shortcomings, "*Alz in einem is nisht du be keinem.*" "No person has every good quality."

Or "*Az me lebdt, derlebtmen.*"—her willingness to hold out for good things to "finally" happen. "If you live long enough, you will live to see it."

"*Gott zoll upitin,*" she would say, to ward off evil spirits, "God should prevent it." This was one of several superstitious holdovers from her otherwise modern life back in Odessa. Like Tuesday is the safe day to embark on a long journey, and one must take a moment before walking out the door to sit on the suitcases for good luck.

"*Überleben,*" she would say, "We went through so much."

"*Überleben.*" It is a German word as well as a Yiddish one. I thought it meant to live through something difficult. But Diane Ackerman, in her book *The Zookeeper's Wife,* when describing the travails of the Jews in the Warsaw Ghetto, wrote that the word means to stay alive and, moreover, to prevail.

If I had needed simply to survive, I might not have made it. I never had the longing to hang on to life for its own sake. Just to live, to be caught in the daily grind, while I dragged my internal struggles along each day. But to prevail, to prove myself more powerful than opposing forces, inspired me. To live an inspired life, a life of meaning, to understand the challenges put before me. This galvanized my spirit—to triumph over hardships, to live the life that is within me. I wanted a glimpse into the essence of my soul's journey.

What exquisite grace guided my way to San Miguel de Allende, a city in the highlands of Mexico?

It began in the most mundane way. I sat at my kitchen table, leafing through an AARP magazine that had arrived in my mailbox earlier that morning. A photo caught my eye—a smiling woman leaning against the railing of a small balcony overlooking a colorful city. I cut out the article of great places in the world to retire and filed it.

Several years later, a friend mentioned that her friend, with whom I had a passing acquaintance, had bought a condominium in a city nestled in a valley in Mexico, a city called San Miguel de Allende. My mind turned to the photo of the woman on the balcony.

"Is this the place?" I asked, showing my friend the article I retrieved from my filing cabinet.

"Yes, it is."

Several months later, I arrived at that condo. I did not know anyone in San Miguel, and for the first week, the only words I spoke were *"Buenos Dias,"* the morning greeting exchanged with passersby in the street. Who could have predicted the rich life that would unfold from this lonely beginning?

Conde Nast Traveler voted San Miguel de Allende the world's best small city for several years running. It is said of San Miguel that first-timers contact a realtor within three days and purchase a home within the first week.

I will leave it to the travel writers to do justice to this beautiful UNESCO World Heritage Site city. Rather, this is my tale of finding refuge in San Miguel —what it has meant in my life, and what living here for four or five months each winter for the past nine years has revealed to me.

I walk around town and say aloud, unable to contain the rush of gratitude I feel, "Oh my God, I can't believe I am living here surrounded by this beauty. I can't believe this is my life." Somehow I have become one of the fortunate ones who is living in a place that is beautiful and suits them, a place that engages all my senses. I have become someone who is enjoying life, whose personal nature and sensibilities are fulfilled. In these moments, I feel I have done life right, I have succeeded.

I love that I need to allocate extra time on my way to a restaurant or concert or food shopping to greet people, to give and receive warmth and affection. I love that the musicians whose performances

I attend, stop and talk for a moment, even make their way across the street to say hello. My visibility is a source of ceaseless wonder. I am not an onlooker. I am a participant. I live in community.

All this, in addition to the delicious aspect of life here that suits me so well—I can walk wherever I want to go. I arrive everywhere on my own power. I am free of cars and endless freeways. As a young girl sitting in my dad's silver Chevrolet Impala, I had felt the cement walls of the Lodge Freeway in Detroit closing in on me, dispiriting and soul shriveling. Here, in the evening, I look at the moon and smell the floral-scented air as I make my way by foot up the incline to my apartment.

Living in San Miguel is one big celebration of life. Color, music, dancing, theater—all walkable, accessible, affordable. Exquisite attention to detail and beauty. Spontaneous joy, people giving themselves to life wholeheartedly. The pleasure centers in my brain undergo an intense workout here in San Miguel, new synapses forming daily. I have given myself the opportunity to partake in the good life.

It is morning, and I walk to Parque Juarez for my morning run, calisthenics, and stair climbing. Every morning—for years. And each time when I enter the park, I sigh a sigh of delicious wellbeing. I am not far away, lost in thought, but am here with the plants and crafted stonework and bird song and flowers and canyons and the butterfly garden. Always, every morning, Parque Juarez is as fresh and new to me as the crisp air generated by all the living green. When my time here on earth is over, I want my ashes strewn down its canyon.

It is December 2016. As I am escorted to my seat in the restaurant, I hear the name of the newly elected President of the United

States at every table I pass. One after another, an extended conversation of dismay ripples through the room. I am among likeminded people. They not only feel as I do but are spending their dinner hour talking about what I need to talk about.

We are ex-pats from the U.S. and Canada. We are of a certain age. So many fascinating life stories to share!

It is after nine o'clock in the evening. I am walking home from the last keynote of the last night of the world-class San Miguel Writer's Conference. It is just a six-minute walk from my apartment to the Hotel Real de Minas where the conference is convened, a world within a world. Writers and poets, whose books I have read, have spent the week with us. My mind and heart are stimulated, inspired, enriched. Every year in February. I take it in; I have given this gift to myself. I have given myself a life that nourishes me.

It is in San Miguel that I found my tribe. High up in the mountains, in this city nestled in a valley, my joy radiates outward, allowing me to become a "people magnet," as my friend Julie calls me. It seems to me we are all magnets pulling one another in with the enthusiasm generated by being here. Our sense of awe at finding ourselves living this life is contagious. Not only are there so many of us likeminded ones, but we live within walking distance of one another and have time to spare which we can spend together.

San Miguel, with its abundant cultural life, attracts artists, intellectuals, children of the 60s, those on a spiritual path. And I find my home with them. It is a richly fertile social laboratory where I can see who I am. To survive and thrive, I needed to face myself on every level, every day—physical, emotional, mental, and spiritual. And the work I dedicated to managing my dysregulated body and challenged emotions has honed me into a substantial woman. I am seasoned and tempered, and I find I have wisdom to offer and kindness to share.

We are gathered at an outdoor concert at El Chorro. In this magical setting, we crane our necks upwards to watch magnificent white migrating birds, egrets, circling high above us among the treetops. Beto, a tall, lanky young Mexican, is playing his clarinet. He is sending his music straight from his heart, waves of vibration pouring out to the celestial spheres. Drawn into the poignant, soul-stirring French melody *"Si Tu Vois Ma Mére,"* I feel a sudden quickening of life within my body. A powerful, previously unknown surge streams through me, a stunning, unfamiliar sensation. "I love life! I love living!"

It turns out my mother's words are true: *"Az me lebdt, derlebtmen."*

I will go on giving my best to life, I tell myself.
As I have always done.

Diana in San Miguel de Allende

Postscript

WHAT HAPPENED NEXT IS INEXPLICABLE.

I wrote to several community centers in Munich, Germany asking for help locating my first father's grave.

Within hours, I received a response from a Chabad rabbi living in Munich, one Rabbi Diskin.

"Sure," he wrote, "I will help you."

We agreed Rabbi Diskin would visit the cemetery where Mendel Weisman is buried. Rabbi Diskin would find the grave and send me photographs of the tombstone. We would then decide if the gravestone needed tending or repair.

Several weeks later, I was stunned to receive this photograph:

The translation is as follows:

> *Buried Here*
> *A good-hearted man*
> *Cut down in the spring of his life*
> *31 years old*
> *a tragic death*
> *Menachem Mendel*
> *son of Mordecai, of blessed memory*
> *Weisman*
> *born in the city of Radom, Poland*
> *died on the 28th day of Tamuz, 1949*
> *"May his soul be bound up in the bond of eternal life"*

The 28th day in the month of Tamuz in the Jewish lunar calendar, corresponds to the date July 25, 1949.

In the text of the chapter, "Father" I describe a slab, flat to the ground, with these words:

> *Mendel Weisman*
> *Geboren: 1918*
> *Tot: July 25, 1949*
> *From Radom, Poland*
> *untimely death*
> *returned to the dust*

The events in the "Father" chapter are not excavated memories—rather, I faithfully recorded all the particulars immediately upon my return from Munich to Tel Aviv in 1976.

The question begs to be answered: which is the legitimate grave and gravestone of Mendel Weisman?

It is reasonable to assume it is the upright tombstone found by Rabbi Diskin, pictured in this Postscript.

Whose then, is the gravestone I wept and prayed over in 1976?

A young man, left behind in a lonely grave, while his fellow Holocaust survivors emigrated from Germany to parts unknown, in search of their post-war lives.

A mystery—unsolved.

Works Cited

Healing Collective Trauma: A Process for Integrating Our Intergenerational and Cultural Wounds. Thomas Hübl, Julie Jordan Avvrit; Sounds True; 2020

The Zookeeper's Wife. Diane Ackerman; W.W. Norton & Company; 2008

Quest for Eternal Sunshine: A Holocaust Survivor's Journey from Darkness to Light. Myra Goodman; She Writes Press; 2020

In the Body of the World. Eve Ensler; Picador, an imprint of Macmillan; 2014

"The Wisdom of Trauma." A film featuring Gabor Maté, produced and directed by Zaya & Maurizio Benazzo, and Caroline Harrison; 2021

Adult Psychiatric Outcomes of Bullying and Being Bullied by Peers in Childhood and Adolescence. William E. Copeland, PhD, Dieter Wolke, PhD; The Journal of the American Medical Association, Psychiatry; 2013

Rilke's Book of Hours: Love Poems to God. Rainer Maria Rilke; Translation by Joanna Macy and Anita Barrows; Riverhead Books; 1996, 2005

Acknowledgments

WRITING *FINDING REFUGE* HAS BEEN a healing and enchanting journey. The writing and all that followed—a magical mystery tour guided by many forces, seen and unseen. I am utterly awed and grateful.

I wish to thank the publishers of this book: Bookmakers Inc: Judyth Hill and Mary Meade.

Judyth Hill, editor and poet extraordinaire—Judyth is unfailingly devoted, authentic, knowledgeable, skillful, and fiery in the name of excellence. She is a formidable force for the good, caring passionately about every word and phrasing, every comma, and quotation mark. What a heartfelt powerhouse to have at and on my side. Judyth, thank you for riding the wave of this intense encounter between us as we birthed my chapters into a polished text.

Mary Meade has been a gentle and soothing presence from the moment we met. She has revealed to me the exquisite artistry necessary to escort a manuscript into a beautifully crafted book. Who knew, definitely not I, all the many choices and aesthetic vision involved in bookmaking. Mary is a master at her craft.

I extend my love and gratitude to my dear friends who read parts of the manuscript when it was a work in progress. Kim Ben-Ezra, Susan Fisher, Marilyn Hoch, and Diane Weber-Shapiro, I am indebted to you for taking the time to read and offer your thoughtful comments and feedback. Included in this list, and with a special thank you and love, are Ellen Akerman, Nadine Gay, and Julie Gellner who went the distance with me—all the way to the finish line. You read and listened, cared and supported me—and I extend a deep bow to you.

Thank you also, dear people, for listening as I read my raw writing aloud to you very early on in the process: Michael Roblee, the lovely women from Group (you know who you are), Karen Altshuler, Barbara Anbender, Deborah Roberts, Cheryl Kandel and Ariella Morrison.

To Judy Wilson and in memory of Gene Humphrey—I can still feel the holy stillness surrounding us in the dusk as you sat listening raptly and I read chapters to you. Thank you for your unfailing kindness and words of encouragement.

Thank you, Jeffrey Rediger, MD, for your wonderful book, *Cured: The Life-Changing Science of Spontaneous Healing;* Flatiron Books; 2020, that taught me the possibility of creating a new neural pathway in forty-five days.

Thank you, Joan Borysenko, PhD, for your book, *Guilt is the Teacher, Love is the Lesson;* Grand Central Publishing; 1991, wherein I first learned about inner child healing.

Thank you so very much, dear Sandra Strauss Schwartz and Michael Wolk, for your kind and generous willingness to proofread this book. Your proofreading was an important contribution to my book.

Thank you, Ellen Seiss, for giving me the date of Ronnie's Bar Mitzvah and getting me started.

Thank you, dear Levinson brothers, Sandy, Marty, and Jay, for giving me permission to use the names and identifying characteristics of your parents and family. I could not have published the chapter "When Sandy Broke His Arm . . ." without your kind permission. Sandy, thank you for being a constant in my life.

To my dear and precious friend Kathleen Goldberg—you are a shining example of one who lives the teachings of the Pathwork with emotional honesty and impeccability. We have navigated the waters of the creation of this book together, deepening and strengthening our friendship all the more, (who thought more was even possible?). You have been my champion, my support, showering me with love, taking in my love for you, mirroring my worth to me. To my dear faithful, heartfelt, gorgeous, and gracious friend—thank you with all my heart.

To Rosa Naparstek—my soul sister. We have had an ongoing conversation for over forty years, often daily, occasionally several times a day. We are children of Holocaust survivors and we are survivors of trauma. We have known one another all our lives. We have matched intellect to intellect. You have listened to me and listened and listened yet again. We have argued and debated. I have been awed by your creative process—your poetry and your artwork. We have grown and evolved as we've shared this journey of life with one another. You have read and re-read and offered your wisdom. Your presence in my life is invaluable.

To Brian O'Donnell, Master Pathwork teacher, who has taught around the globe in China, Japan, Brazil, Argentina, Italy, Israel, and across the U.S.—it is you who gave me the language and the insights. "Breaking the Spell" are your words. "Introjecting the negative projection" is your teaching. In your refined, patrician, generous and stalwart manner, you have been my pillar. You are the ultimate exemplar of living the Pathwork teachings. You embody them. You are impeccable. I respect you with all my heart. Thank you, thank you, thank you. Unfailing gratitude and much love to you.

To Nancy Judge, Healing Touch Practitioner—I have been healing physically, emotionally, mentally, and spiritually due to the weekly Healing Touch treatments you have bestowed upon me for twenty years and more. I feel deeply grateful to you for your work. And—I feel humbled by your unfailing kindness and generosity. You give without ego, without an agenda, without expecting something in return. Knowing you is humbling, proof that kindness like yours does exist in this world. And you gave me a life-altering teaching. I use it every day, several times a day. It is my touchstone—"Release others' fears and limitations. Think your own loving thoughts." How these words bring me up short when I am reactive and judgmental. How excruciatingly I need to stretch, stretch, to even begin to live by them. But what freedom and respite when I am able! Thank you Nancy—love and a deep bow to you.

To my brother Sam Kuper—you definitely did not ask to be the brother of a memoirist. Your sensibility and sense of privacy would never have allowed the sharing of our parents' lives as I have done in my book. Nevertheless—I know this has been difficult for you and I am grateful all the more for it—you have graciously stood by me as I brought this memoir to life. I know it is love that has motivated you—your abiding love for me. Underneath all our personality and lifestyle differences—we share enduring love for one another. We do what it takes to build bridges across our divides and to uphold the honor of being brother and sister. I am eternally grateful for you and love you dearly.

To Laurie Kuper, my sister-in-law—thank you for understanding and supporting me, for your love, your friendship, and your listening. Thank you for keeping the home fires burning. Much love from me to you.

To my precious son Raphele, Raphael Baruch Kuper—what unseen hand brought us together in this lifetime? How did we ever find one another? Are you connected somehow to the spirit of Soolinka, as was once revealed to me in a vision? We had challenging conditions in the beginning and we both have given our best. You have grown into a man with a full life, a successful career, and a solid marriage to my beautiful daughter-in-law, Kevia Wright. I raise a toast to you both—intrepid skiers, snowboarders, world travelers, adventurers. I am very proud of both of you. My daily heartfelt prayer is for your good health and safety. With much love always, Mom.

Thank you to all my dear ones, seen and unseen, from the bottom of my heart, for everything, for more than I can possibly say.

About the Author

DIANA KUPER IS A GRADUATE of the University of Michigan, Tel Aviv University, and the Merrill-Palmer Institute (now The Michigan School of Psychology). During her seven-year residence in Israel, she counseled adults for the Community Mental Health Center in Jaffa and facilitated support groups for the Ministry of Defense.

Diana Kuper is a psychotherapist in private practice, counseling individuals, couples, and groups. She has taught courses on the psychology of women and classes for women—"Regarding Relationships."

She is grateful for her writerly imagination, which has sustained her throughout her life.

Diana Kuper divides her time between Michigan and San Miguel de Allende.

Finding Refuge is her first book.